T0094476

Eternal Hydra

Anton Piatigorsky

Coach House Books, Toronto

first edition

For production enquiries, please contact Michael Petrasek, Kensington
Literary Representation, kensingtonlit@rogers.com or 416 979 0187.

Published with the generous assistance of the Canada Council for the
Arts and the Ontario Arts Council. Coach House Books also acknowl-
edges the support of the Government of Ontario through the Ontario
Book Publishing Tax Credit and the Government of Canada through
the Book Publishing Industry Development Program.

LIBRARY AND ARCHIVES CANADA CATALOGUING IN PUBLICATION

Piatigorsky, Anton, 1972-
    Eternal hydra / Anton Piatigorsky. -- 1st ed.

ISBN 978-1-55245-201-1
7   I. Title.
7PS8581.I218E83 2009   C812'.6   C2009-902646-5

In loving memory of Stephen J. Roth

Production History

Eternal Hydra was commissioned by the Stratford Festival of Canada.

A one-act version of the play premiered on July 13, 2002, in the festival's Studio Theatre. The cast and crew were as follows.

Vivian Ezra/Gwendolyn Jackson: Chick Reid
Randall Wellington, Jr./Randall Wellington, Sr.:
    Paul Soles
Gordias Carbuncle: Stephen Ouimette
Pauline Newberry/Selma Thomas: Karen Robinson

Director: Andrey Tarasiuk
Production Dramaturg: Roy Surette
Set Designer: Lorenzo Savoini
Costume Designer: Joanne Dente
Lighting Designer: Robert Thomson
Sound Design: Peter McBoyle
Assistant Lighting Designer: Wendy Greenwood
Stage Manager: Michael Hart
Assistant Stage Manager: Allison Spearin
Production Stage Manager: Michael Hart

The full-length version was given a workshop production by Crow's Theatre in November of 2007.

The Crow's Theatre production premiered at Buddies in Bad Times Theatre on May 21, 2009, with the following cast and crew.

Vivian Ezra/Gwendolyn Jackson/Sarah Briggs:
   Liisa Repo-Martell
Randall Wellington, Jr./Randall Wellington, Sr./Léon LaBas:
   Sam Malkin
Gordias Carbuncle/Henry Warmoth: David Ferry
Pauline Newberry/Selma Thomas/Narrator: Karen Robinson

Director: Chris Abraham
Set and Lighting Designer: John Thompson
Costume Designer: Barbara Rowe
Sound Design: Richard Feren
Producer: Gillian Hards
Associate Producer: Mark Aikman
Production Manager: Mathew Byrne
Stage Manager: Merissa Tordjman

Characters

Vivian Ezra: a scholar
Randall Wellington, Jr.: a publisher
Gordias Carbuncle: a writer
Pauline Newberry: a writer
Gwendolyn Jackson: a scholar
Selma Thomas: a writer
Randall Wellington, Sr.: a publisher
Narrator: a shoemaker
Léon LaBas: a shop owner
Henry Warmoth: a carpetbagger
Sarah Briggs: a socialite

There are four actors, cast as follows:

Vivian Ezra/Gwendolyn Jackson/Sarah Briggs
Wellington Jr./Wellington Sr./Léon LaBas
Gordias Carbuncle/Henry Warmoth
Pauline Newberry/Selma Thomas/Narrator

Act One

(*Vivian Ezra stands alone, holding a large manuscript. She directly addresses the audience.*)

EZRA: Genius is dead, I said. There's no godlike, authorial figure behind the writing of a book. The great modernist writer doesn't always 'write' in the classical sense at all. Often he relies on extensive source materials. That's why every important author needs a definitive editor. A professional scholar is best. I am that editor and scholar for Gordias Carbuncle.

(*A wealthy publisher, Randall Wellington, sits behind his desk. He leans back in his chair, intrigued.*)

Randall Wellington didn't need my introduction. But I wanted to make a good impression on this intelligent and tasteful publisher. A man who knows the meaning of art. I mean, look, here, at his office.

(*Ezra indicates a coffee table with an African statue on it.*) A Kasai-Sankuru figure from the Eastern Pende peoples. Warm. Unpretentious.

(*She indicates two paintings: a Picasso, an Arika.*) Two oil paintings in understated frames. The Picasso, bought at auction from the collection of a late baroness. The Arika portrait of Samuel Beckett was a gift from the artist.

(*She indicates a bookshelf, filled with volumes.*) Bookshelf: handmade, oak. All first editions. Hemingway, Woolf, Faulkner. Most are signed by their respective authors.

(*She indicates a Persian rug.*) A Persian pile, Sehna knots, perhaps one thousand per square inch. An arabesque design almost entirely done in silk. I suspect it's from Kashan.

(*She indicates a window.*) His view of Central Park. That copper roof in the distance is a slice of the Plaza.

Here, in this office, I made my declaration: I am Vivian Ezra, Gordias Carbuncle's representative. And I'm here to entwine my name forever with his. Forever, because of this ...

(*She holds the manuscript.*) Clutching the manuscript, I stood before Wellington.

WELLINGTON: Let's cut to the chase.

EZRA: (*out*) He said.

WELLINGTON: You've got *Eternal Hydra?*

EZRA: I do.

WELLINGTON: That's not possible. It's gone, lost, kaput.

EZRA: Not anymore, it's not.
(*out*) Then he looked at his watch.

(*Wellington is looking at his watch.*)

I'm sorry, it's clearly not a good time ...

WELLINGTON: No, no ...

EZRA: I'll come back ... I should come back.

WELLINGTON: It's fine! It's nothing!

EZRA: I can come back.

WELLINGTON: Please. Relax.

(*Ezra sits.*)

Eternal Hydra …

EZRA: You've heard of it, I'm sure.

WELLINGTON: Yes. My father's project.

EZRA: There are ninety-nine distinct chapters. He intended one hundred, but it seems the final chapter was never written. The novel's composed of a series of first-person monologues. Different voices, from every corner of the world.

WELLINGTON: Like Carbuncle's Moroccan stories?

EZRA: Similar, but with greater unity. There's a hidden protagonist. A different character in each chapter who –

WELLINGTON: Yes.

EZRA: (*out*) He interrupted.

WELLINGTON: Must be long.

EZRA: Almost a thousand pages.

WELLINGTON: I'd like to see it.

EZRA: No. (*Pause.*) I mean … that depends …

(*Wellington growls in thought.*)

(*out*) He made a sound that couldn't be good.

WELLINGTON: My father used to say that Gordias Carbuncle could've been one of the twentieth century's greatest writers.

EZRA: Did he really?

WELLINGTON: 'If only his book wasn't lost!'

EZRA: Well, I don't think you'll be disappointed.

(*Wellington looks at his watch.*)

(*out*) The watch, again. Bad sign. He wants to get to the point. The name Carbuncle's a pseudonym, of course. His parents were Irish Jews. Born and raised in Dublin. He drank too much, died of liver failure on the day the Germans invaded Paris. Tragic. He was an exceptional man. A biting wit, great probity, genuine kindness and charm.

WELLINGTON: You've taken a liking to him.

EZRA: Well, yes, I suppose I have.
  (*out*) What I didn't tell him, then, was that the late Gordias Carbuncle lives with me at home. He first appeared in my dreams over five years ago, then extracted from my dreamscape and materialized in my life. Now, we walk together, talk together, jest and work and play, all our waking hours. Here he is, just now.

(*Gordias Carbuncle appears.*)

CARBUNCLE: Vivian Ezra!

EZRA: Ah, Gordias. Those ridiculous suits, that fabulous smile. Sometimes we huddle all night together while he whispers poetry in my ear. Sweet lines from *Eternal Hydra*. We take our long autumnal walks on the train tracks outside Providence. I will never get bored of this man.

CARBUNCLE: I don't like the way he sits.

(*Wellington looks at his watch.*)

The way he always checks his watch. Why's he checking his watch?

EZRA: He runs this whole place. He's very strapped for time.

CARBUNCLE: Do we bore him? Am I a bore? You're certain he's the best?

EZRA: Wellington and Company's the smartest publisher around. As it was with his father.

CARBUNCLE: It's one of our nomenclature's nasty truths that the namesake son of a great man remains a 'junior' all his life. For the borrowing of a name is like the borrowing of a soul; there is tainting in transaction. That ineffable mysterium within the original man is somehow lost in transit, leaving the second man inferior, a mere copy, a golem of sorts. I think we should leave.

11

EZRA: (*out*) Carbuncle had me worried. Perhaps I'd misjudged Randall Jr.

(*Wellington looks at his watch.*)

WELLINGTON: You were saying ...

EZRA: Yes.
(*She takes a deep breath, looks to Carbuncle.*) I'm interested in publishing the first edition of *Eternal Hydra*. I've been working on it, now, for almost six years. I've written a lengthy introduction, with notes and commentary.

WELLINGTON: You've had his book for six years?

EZRA: I'd like to discuss terms. I have a letter of permission from Carbuncle's sole remaining relative.

WELLINGTON: Great.

EZRA: I can't go below twenty percent. And I need a reasonable advance to compensate my labour.

CARBUNCLE: The budget! The budget!

EZRA: Oh, and a high-priority promotions budget. These terms are non-negotiable.

WELLINGTON: Miss Ezra ...

EZRA: You can call me Vivian.

WELLINGTON: Vivian, I don't think anybody in the history of this firm has ever gotten twenty percent.

EZRA: It's not for me, you understand. I have in mind a foundation for the further study of Carbuncle's –

WELLINGTON: Okay, wait.

EZRA: (*out*) He interrupted.

WELLINGTON: I'm sure you know that Wellington and Company's no longer a family-run business. We have a parent company –

CARBUNCLE: Mother of a still-born martyr!

EZRA: What are you saying?

WELLINGTON: – and we're under certain pressures …

CARBUNCLE: Draw and quarter the cur! Pluck off the bastard's toes!

EZRA: Look, if your parent company needs a sensational headline of some sort, there's plenty of intrigue here. A genuine mystery around how the novel was lost in the first place. I believe it was a wilful act of deceit –

WELLINGTON: Vivian …

EZRA: You see, in 1940, the manuscript was entrusted to Gwendolyn Jackson, an expatriate British scholar –

WELLINGTON: Jackson.

EZRA: Who already had a quite complicated relationship to –

WELLINGTON: I've heard of her.

EZRA: Which I think implies some malicious –

WELLINGTON: She just died.

EZRA: That's right. I was worried about approaching until –

WELLINGTON: My father was in her will.

EZRA: He was?

WELLINGTON: She wrote it thirty years ago. Willed him a box of papers. We just got it last week.

EZRA: (*out*) I was beyond thrilled.
     Do you think that we might –

WELLINGTON: Sure, I'll call Jenna.

CARBUNCLE: That Jackson woman was an unbelievable bore.

EZRA: It's possible she had something else that you wrote.

CARBUNCLE: But I'm here to answer all your queries.

WELLINGTON: (*into the speaker phone*) Jenna, could you send in my one-thirty? Oh, and please bring in that box from the Jackson estate.

EZRA: I have to look.

WELLINGTON: (*into the speaker*) It's in overstock. In the back.

EZRA: Who knows what other treasures she had in her possession?

WELLINGTON: I assume *Eternal Hydra* needs to be read with a stack of references. Encyclopedia, the OED.

CARBUNCLE: You mean it's the type of book that made this firm famous.

EZRA: *Eternal Hydra* can be studied or simply enjoyed.

CARBUNCLE: Or worshipped, if one were inclined.

WELLINGTON: The modern reader's online, in the car, on the beach, picking the kids up from school. Not quite as interested in conjuring pantheons with every word.

EZRA: But for the small, avid audience. And the historical importance, you must admit –

WELLINGTON: My father's old commissions, that's not what I'm doing for this company.

CARBUNCLE: Traitor! Unnatural rebel!

EZRA: You clearly don't want it.

WELLINGTON: No, I never said –

EZRA: Thanks for your time, Mr. Wellington.

(*She stands and starts to exit.*)

CARBUNCLE: Vivian!

EZRA: We're negotiating, Gordias. We have to be ready to walk.

WELLINGTON: Hang on a minute. I want you to meet someone.

CARBUNCLE: You won't get your foundation! I'll never amount to anything!

EZRA: We can't be in any kind of rush.

(*Carbuncle tries to calm down. Ezra takes his hand.*)

CARBUNCLE: My sweet, sweet Juno, I can't wait any longer …

(*He kisses Ezra's hand.*)

EZRA: Don't say that.

CARBUNCLE: It's been decades. What if my novel's worthless?

EZRA: It's a masterpiece, my Jove. Every bit as good as –

CARBUNCLE: Toilet tissue for a diarrheic hippopotamus in the middle of the mud-soaked upper Nile.

(*Ezra laughs.*)

WELLINGTON: What's funny?

EZRA: I'm sorry?

WELLINGTON: You were laughing.

EZRA: I was thinking of *Eternal Hydra*. One of the novel's ninety-nine voices is from ancient Egypt. A slave serving young king Tutankhamen. He's being put to death, to accompany King Tut in the underworld. As he's dying – it's a very funny bit – he has this perverted obsession with a little cat …

WELLINGTON: Uh-huh. (*Pause.*) Listen, I want you to meet Pauline Newberry. She's one of my favourite writers.

EZRA: The novelist?

WELLINGTON: When I heard you'd something new on Carbuncle I arranged your meetings back to back.

EZRA: What's her book? A few years ago?

WELLINGTON: *Major Street.*

EZRA: That's right.

WELLINGTON: Shortlisted for the Pulitzer. You two share some common ground.

NEWBERRY: Hello?
    (*Newberry enters, carrying the box.*) Randall …

WELLINGTON: Pauline …

NEWBERRY: Where should I put this thing?

WELLINGTON: Why the hell didn't Jenna bring it in herself?

NEWBERRY: I told her I'd do it.

EZRA: (*out*) I couldn't wait to open that box.

(*Newberry puts the box down.*)

WELLINGTON: You look great.

NEWBERRY: No, I'm frazzled. Nathaniel decides, this morning, to see if his animals can swim. In the toilet. Just as I'm leaving.

WELLINGTON: Of course.

EZRA: Nathaniel?

(*Newberry looks at Ezra.*)

NEWBERRY: My son. He's two.

EZRA: Oh.

NEWBERRY: Hello.

WELLINGTON: Pauline Newberry, Vivian Ezra.

NEWBERRY: Nice to meet you.

EZRA: Yes.

CARBUNCLE: Never mind me, of course.

EZRA: Do you think that we could, maybe, look inside that –

WELLINGTON: We're publishing Pauline's second novel this fall. Historical fiction. A fine book.

EZRA: Really?

NEWBERRY: Mm-hm. Working out the final details today.

WELLINGTON: Vivian's here looking to publish a certain manuscript that might be of interest to you.

NEWBERRY: Really?

EZRA: (*out*) It was an awkward moment. I wasn't going to tell this stranger about *Eternal Hydra*.

CARBUNCLE: You mean, until the moment's right.

NEWBERRY: You're a novelist?

EZRA: Uh, no. A scholar.

WELLINGTON: Vivian's an up-and-comer in comp. lit. at Brown. Her specialty's twentieth century. Modernism, mostly. Teaches a magnificent course on Proust, Joyce, Faulkner. Or so I've been told.

NEWBERRY: I think I've heard of you.

EZRA: (*out*) For Chrissakes, she's never heard of me.

NEWBERRY: Your lectures on *The Sound and The Fury* made a big impression on a friend of mine.

EZRA: Really? Oh. Well, it's one of my favourites ...

CARBUNCLE: One of your favourites, is it?

EZRA: Not my absolute favourite, of course.

NEWBERRY: You have an absolute favourite? Please, do tell!

(*Wellington and Newberry laugh.*)

CARBUNCLE: Well? There's my moment. I need no grander introduction!

WELLINGTON: Tell us about your book. But skip the pretty details, okay? I've got about twenty minutes.

NEWBERRY: Ah, Randall ...
        (*to Ezra*) He was way more pleasant when he was trying to impress me.

WELLINGTON: Those days are long gone, Pauline.

NEWBERRY: The novel's called *Scribbled Away*. It takes place in Paris, during the thirties. The protagonist's a young fiction writer based on an actual historical figure. A woman named

Selma Thomas. She was an unknown African-American expat from Louisiana. She hung out on the periphery with Senghor, Césaire, all the budding Négritude writers. You've heard of them?

EZRA: The French colonial inheritors of the Harlem Renaissance. (*out*) Have I heard of them, she asks! I'm a scholar in the field!

NEWBERRY: She was part of that whole circle. Selma Thomas was more sophisticated, in my opinion. Ahead of her time. She had it rough, no money, rundown apartment. It was tough, Paris those years …

EZRA: I know about Paris in the thirties.

WELLINGTON: Tell her about Carbuncle.

CARBUNCLE: I beg your pardon?

NEWBERRY: One of my minor characters is a lesser-known modernist, quite a complicated man actually, who befriended Selma Thomas. Named Gordias Carbuncle.

WELLINGTON: See?

NEWBERRY: His work's hardly known. Several short stories – the best are set in Morocco – and one slim novella called *Buttress Down*. He wrote a mammoth novel, *Eternal Hydra*, that's been lost for sixty years. No one can find it. It was brilliant, supposedly.

CARBUNCLE: Oh, it's brilliant, my dear!

NEWBERRY: You look surprised.

WELLINGTON: Vivian has come to me in order to publish *Eternal Hydra*.

EZRA: No, Mr. Wellington, please ...

WELLINGTON: Right there, under her arm!

NEWBERRY: You're kidding.

EZRA: I'd rather not –

NEWBERRY: That's fantastic!

CARBUNCLE: Aha!

NEWBERRY: Can I see it?

CARBUNCLE: A fan!

NEWBERRY: How did you get it?

(*Ezra hesitates.*)

EZRA: Gordias?

CARBUNCLE: Tell her, Vivian. The cat's out of the bag.

EZRA: I was in Paris, researching my first book, based on my dissertation. Lesser-known expatriate writers between the wars. One day, I visited the apartment of an aging scholar named Gwendolyn Jackson.

WELLINGTON: She just died.

EZRA: Jackson was in her mid-nineties when I met her, quite senile. She let me have a chest of her papers, an astonishing wealth of documents, original copies of *transition*, programs from the Cirque Medrano. The manuscript was there. *Eternal Hydra*, in its entirety.

NEWBERRY: That's incredible.

EZRA: Obviously buried, and wilfully, too. Spiteful woman. Can you imagine? Stealing a masterpiece and stashing it away from the world? Should be a criminal offence.

CARBUNCLE: Spiteful and jealous, that's what she was.

EZRA: Thank God for her senility. I don't think she realized what she gave me.

WELLINGTON: Probably meant it for my father.

EZRA: At least now she's dead.

NEWBERRY: Why'd she hide the book?

CARBUNCLE: Too many times I spurned her offers of romance.

EZRA: She was jealous. Controlling. A case of unrequited love. She snatched the novel when he unexpectedly died, before anyone knew its location. This is June of 1940, the Nazis invading Paris. People had other things on their mind.

NEWBERRY: Amazing …

CARBUNCLE: Tragic.

EZRA: So the story goes. At least that's what he told me.

WELLINGTON: Told you?

CARBUNCLE: Whoops.

EZRA: I … inferred. From what I read …

WELLINGTON: I see …

EZRA: Did I say 'told me'?

WELLINGTON: You did.

CARBUNCLE: You bet.

EZRA: How silly.

NEWBERRY: I'd kill to read that book.

EZRA: Well, when Wellington and Company agrees to my terms …

(*Newberry looks to Wellington.*)

WELLINGTON: (*to Newberry*) Twenty percent.

(*Newberry laughs.*)

EZRA: *Eternal Hydra*'s the culmination of an entire life's work!

WELLINGTON: Doesn't matter if it's the third part of the goddamn Bible trilogy, I can't give you twenty percent.

NEWBERRY: It's never done.

CARBUNCLE: Fifteen?

WELLINGTON: I can offer you ten percent with $25,000 in advance, payable in thirds: signing, delivery, publication.

EZRA: Oh.

WELLINGTON: Plus great advertising and distribution – which unfortunately means nothing until the stores decide to shelve it – but I'll bet we can get some pretty big hype on this one. Decent sales to libraries and academics like yourself. All depends on word of mouth.

EZRA: Gordias?

CARBUNCLE: Goddammit. All right.

WELLINGTON: So?

NEWBERRY: Congratulations!

EZRA: Yes. Thank you.

WELLINGTON: Now, here's the thing. I'd be absolutely insane not to tie these two books together. It's nothing really, Pauline, just – assuming you both approve – I was thinking when your novel comes out we could get you on some talk shows together, maybe some readings or panels, hyping the Carbuncle character.

EZRA: You want me to hype her book?

NEWBERRY: Randall, with all due respect, Carbuncle's not –

WELLINGTON: Vivian knows the period better than anyone.

NEWBERRY: My novel's not just about the period.

EZRA: (*out*) I couldn't stand the idea. For us to risk our reputations on this Newberry woman's novel!
    I'm not sure Pauline wants me to do it.

NEWBERRY: It's just … without a specialty on black writers …

EZRA: I've done a couple long chapters on Négritude.

NEWBERRY: That's not really my point.

WELLINGTON: It's a great opportunity.

NEWBERRY: It would have to be in the framework of a larger discussion on Selma Thomas –

WELLINGTON: Of course. And I'm only talking about a few events.

NEWBERRY: Well, in theory, I suppose …

WELLINGTON: Vivian?

EZRA: I can't do it, Gordias!

WELLINGTON: Hello?

EZRA: I'm thinking!

CARBUNCLE: I know it's distasteful. You only want what's best for me. But perhaps it is my fate. To hitch my own enormous prospects, like some hobo's boxcar, to another person's engine. To serve historical fiction, a mere shadow of myself. Famous because this young woman's novel boasts my name in its dramatis personae. Not for my own writing, no ...

EZRA: Not to you! I can't!

CARBUNCLE: A side character! Like a plate of chips to partner the fried cod!

WELLINGTON: Think about it for a few days if you like ...

CARBUNCLE: Accept the offer. Promote her book to the best of your abilities. My own work will follow soon enough.

EZRA: I accept the offer.

WELLINGTON: Excellent!

EZRA: But only if her book is good.

NEWBERRY: Oh, my book's good.

(*Wellington grabs a galley proof from his desk.*)

WELLINGTON: Here's a galley. Have a look.

(*He hands it to Ezra. She starts to flip through it.*)

CARBUNCLE: Where's the part about me?

EZRA: Where's the part about Carbuncle?

NEWBERRY: Let me see.
(*She takes the book, looks through it briefly.*) Here. I'll read it.

EZRA: (*out*) And then Pauline Newberry read us her prose.

NEWBERRY: (*reading*) Chapter six. Five a.m. and the sun's rising over the sixth arrondisement. Selma's stumbling down Rue de Rennes, a little bit tipsy, a lot hungry, alcohol stained on her shirt. She wonders who's awake at this ungodly hour. No slurring revellers left in the sleepy cafés of Montparnasse. Who, then? She bites a nail. Gordias Carbuncle, that's who. He's probably drunk, crooning love songs in his gaudy three-piece suit, or scribbling away on his endless *Hydra*. Selma decides to pay him a visit.

WELLINGTON: I love this scene.

NEWBERRY: (*reading*) She rings the bell at 7 Rue de Fleurus, a block from the Jardin du Luxembourg. Carbuncle buzzes her in without inquiry. Odd man, Selma thinks. Never asks who's dropping by, anytime, any day. She climbs the steep steps to his dingy fourth-floor apartment. His door's ajar. Selma hears him coughing from inside.

CARBUNCLE: Not actually true, that. I was never cavalier. And I never cough.

NEWBERRY: (*reading*) She helps herself to an entrance.

(*The world of Newberry's novel arises. Carbuncle takes off his jacket, untucks his shirt, adopts a hangover. He performs the actions as Newberry reads.*)

Hello? Anybody home?
　　(*reading*) Selma says. Carbuncle looks up from his table. The room is full of smoke. There are papers strewn on the floor, others crumpled on dirty dishes. He's nursing a near empty bottle of Tullamore Dew. He stands, slicks back his scalp, tucks in his fraying shirt. He smiles generously, hoping to cover any sign of debauchery or exhaustion. He bows with the thin shadow of a chivalry almost forgotten.

EZRA: (*mumbling*) 'A chivalry almost forgotten'!

NEWBERRY: (*reading*) Three years she's lived in Paris, but still Selma warms with pride when a white man stands and bows as she enters a room.

(*Newberry enters the world of the novel. She puts down the book. Her 'reading' is now a narration for Ezra and Wellington, with hints of a direct audience address. Her other lines are Selma Thomas's.*)

CARBUNCLE: Selma Thomas! What good fortune! A fresh Georgia peach falls right into my room!

NEWBERRY: I'm from Louisiana.

CARBUNCLE: You are? My apologies.

NEWBERRY: (*out*) Selma, an American at heart, likes to cut to the chase.
I'm hungry.

CARBUNCLE: That's why you've come to your Carbuncle?
(*He grabs two dirty glasses, rubs them on his trousers. He fills them both with Tullamore Dew.*) I only eat with those who agree to drink with me.

NEWBERRY: (*out*) A strange mix, Selma thinks. European formality combined with slovenly attire.

(*Carbuncle bows his head as he hands her the whiskey glass.*)

CARBUNCLE: I'm quite hungry, myself.

NEWBERRY: You should eat your trousers.

CARBUNCLE: I beg your pardon?

NEWBERRY: Your food's stained into them.

CARBUNCLE: Ah, yes. Very true. But surely they're not as tasty as a fresh Georgia peach.

NEWBERRY: I'm from Louisiana.

(*They eye each other curiously as they hold up glasses for a toast.*)

CARBUNCLE: To Selma.

NEWBERRY: To Gordias.

(*They drink together.*)

CARBUNCLE: I have smoked fish and brie. And an almost-fresh baguette.

NEWBERRY: I can eat that.

CARBUNCLE: Then you shall.

NEWBERRY: Thanks.

(*Carbuncle exits.*)

(*out*) Alone now, slowly sobering, she eyes Carbuncle's table. Between the crumpled papers and empty bottles, there's a page, half-written, and on it a silver fountain pen.
   You were writing …

CARBUNCLE: (*off*) No, no, nothing.

NEWBERRY: (*out*) He calls out from the kitchen.

CARBUNCLE: (*off*) Not important at all.

(*Carbuncle returns with a tray of food.*)

NEWBERRY: I'm sorry to disturb you.

CARBUNCLE: No, it's a great relief.

NEWBERRY: (*out*) He puts the tray on his present writing, his face flushing red.

    (*out*) Selma rips a hunk of bread and knives the cheese with its crust. By the time her host steps back, the bread's already crunching in her mouth. Carbuncle's awestruck at her audacity: half horrified, half ecstatic.

(*Newberry puts bread in her mouth and chews.*)

NEWBERRY: (*chewing*) Sorry. I've got no manners.

CARBUNCLE: No, I … it's …

NEWBERRY: (*out*) She loves playing the rude American. Europeans find it thrilling. With a brash foreigner in the room, they release their omnipresent formality.

CARBUNCLE: It looks like you've been on the town.

NEWBERRY: Yeah.

CARBUNCLE: Montmartre?

NEWBERRY: Bricktop's for a while then the Flea Pit after hours.

CARBUNCLE: Dancing your jungle music?

NEWBERRY: I drank my money away.

CARBUNCLE: You can always come to me. More whiskey?

NEWBERRY: Always.

(*He pours drinks for both of them.*)

You're melancholy tonight.

CARBUNCLE: Not really, no.

NEWBERRY: What, then?

CARBUNCLE: Nothing important. Just ... it's a wonder to me.

NEWBERRY: (*out*) He says.

CARBUNCLE: How you write such beautiful fiction drinking the way you do.

NEWBERRY: You do the same.

CARBUNCLE: You drink me under the table, still you're up at eight a.m. And then your words, so beautiful ...

NEWBERRY: I'm nothing special.

CARBUNCLE: You have a rare type of genius.

EZRA: (*mumbling*) He doesn't believe in genius!

NEWBERRY: (*out*) She had reluctantly given him stories only two weeks before. He returned a note effusive with praise. Of course she didn't believe it. She suspected a leniency in his judgment. Not unusual from white artists. They pander to her talents simply because her skin is black. But here, in person, Carbuncle speaks with crumbling sadness. Is it possible?

Selma wonders. Has her fiction, in fact, touched him, for real, on its own terms?

CARBUNCLE: And I thought the Negro mind was a mere repository of Id: all fire and passion and whim. There's plenty of that, of course. Animal lust in your stories. But there's also great structure, irony, authentic voice. Remarkable to read.

NEWBERRY: Authentic voice ...

CARBUNCLE: Yes, I know it. Your writing burns with exotic flare. It hungers with the mysterious longing of a savage continent. The beating rhythms of the tom-tom drum. Very exciting, very new.
(*He pours himself another drink.*) You have the true voice of the Negro.

NEWBERRY: (*out*) Selma clenches her jaw in a swirl of horror, pride, resentment. An exotic animal caged by Gordias Carbuncle. A precious ebony figure displayed in his Musée des Colonies.
True voice of the Negro ...

CARBUNCLE: Yes.

NEWBERRY: True voice of the Irish Jew.

CARBUNCLE: I'm sorry?

NEWBERRY: It's what the Germans say about you. You've got Jew essence, through and through.

CARBUNCLE: I suppose they do.

NEWBERRY: Are they right? After all, from my perspective you're the one who's completely foreign.

EZRA: (*mumbling*) That's contemporary! She'd never say that in the 1930s!

CARBUNCLE: You cannot deny there's an essence to your race.

NEWBERRY: If there's a black essence, there's a Jewish one too.

CARBUNCLE: Yes, there is. An essence bookish, proud and clever. We are the erudite nomads. Exemplified by Gordias Carbuncle, a nomadic stylist, borrowing my hundred voices from every nation and race of the world, just as my parents' people adapted themselves to the hostile homelands of Moors and Catholics, Celts and Slavs, Arabs and Anglicans.
(*He drinks.*) A Jew essence, yes.
(*He picks up the food tray.*) Now if only I were a better writer.

(*He exits with the food.*)

NEWBERRY: (*out*) Selma's block of icy anger suddenly moistens, begins to melt.
What did you say?

CARBUNCLE: (*off*) Have a drink, Selma. Please.

NEWBERRY: You're a great writer, Gordias. God, you're ... I don't even know where to begin –

(*Carbuncle re-enters.*)

CARBUNCLE: Begin by having another drink.

(*He pours her a drink.*)

NEWBERRY: I'm nothing. A big black nobody. All I do is complain about race.

CARBUNCLE: It's magnificent art.

NEWBERRY: It's not literature. No one wants to read it.

CARBUNCLE: Nor do they want to read about the lives of dirty Jews.

NEWBERRY: Always race. No choice.

CARBUNCLE: At least you've talent. I'm nothing but pathetic bravado.

NEWBERRY: That's not true.

CARBUNCLE: Have your drink.

NEWBERRY: No more than me. It's the same.

CARBUNCLE: Stop talking, Selma. Drink.

(*She drinks.*)

Now, as I recall, we were discussing your wonderful writing. What are you looking at?

NEWBERRY: Nothing.

CARBUNCLE: Nothing?

NEWBERRY: I'm just looking.

CARBUNCLE: Is that so?

NEWBERRY: What? I'm not allowed to look?

CARBUNCLE: You're allowed.

NEWBERRY: All right, then.

CARBUNCLE: Look away.

NEWBERRY: I am looking.

CARBUNCLE: Very well. My perfect Georgia peach.

NEWBERRY: I'm from Louisiana.

(*Newberry and Carbuncle move in for a kiss. Ezra stops them.*)

EZRA: No!

(*Ezra stands. Carbuncle and Newberry step out of the novel.*)

WELLINGTON: What?

EZRA: I'm sorry, that's not right. That's not Gordias Carbuncle.

NEWBERRY: Jesus Christ …

WELLINGTON: He's a fictional character.

EZRA: Based on a real person!

NEWBERRY: That neither of us have met.

CARBUNCLE: Speak for yourself, Miss Newberry.

(*Wellington continues as Ezra speaks with Carbuncle, their lines overlapping.*)

EZRA: (*aside to Carbuncle*) You sounded like a racist.

WELLINGTON: Pauline researched her novel for almost three years.

NEWBERRY: Three and a half years …

CARBUNCLE: (*aside to Ezra*) She gave me the words. I felt compelled.

WELLINGTON: Three and a half!

EZRA: (*aside to Carbuncle*) You embarrassed yourself with that display. You embarrassed me.

WELLINGTON: She brings that knowledge to her characters.

CARBUNCLE: (*aside to Ezra*) I'm sorry, Vivian. I let myself get carried away. It was beautifully read; she gave me lines.

EZRA: You're too hungry for recognition.

WELLINGTON: Vivian?

EZRA: What?

WELLINGTON: You with me?

EZRA: Of course.
(*out*) I was frayed, losing composure.
I'm sorry, that's ... your writing, the words you give him, they have absolutely no relation to Gordias Carbuncle. None whatsoever.

NEWBERRY: It's an accurate portrait of the man I studied.

EZRA: It isn't him! All those Negro stereotypes. All that stuff about 'tom-tom drums.'

NEWBERRY: You know as well as I do, Parisian men of the 1930s exoticized the hell out of black Americans.

EZRA: Gordias Carbuncle was fifty years ahead of his time!

NEWBERRY: Josephine Baker. The Colonial Exposition of 1931 –

EZRA: He wrote beautiful passages on cultural construction. You'll see when you read *Eternal Hydra*.

WELLINGTON: Okay, time out, both of you.

(*Ezra steps away.*)

EZRA: (*out*) I looked out the window and tried to calm down.
(*She takes a deep breath.*) (*out*) How dare she steal this great man!

CARBUNCLE: Don't think of it as theft. Rather, conflicting visions. There's great currency in mystery.

NEWBERRY: Look, maybe you're right. Maybe Carbuncle's views on race were more complex than those around him. But my novel's the portrait of an era. Parisian exoticism is essential.

EZRA: He's not a tool for some agenda.

NEWBERRY: It's Selma Thomas's perspective. A black American woman living in Europe. A triple outsider. She has unique insight into the intricate social mores of the time, the genius posturing, the desperate defences of white Parisians.

EZRA: Never mind Carbuncle has none of those defences.

NEWBERRY: Everyone in the book is portrayed with common humanity.

EZRA: Oh, Christ …

NEWBERRY: It's the quality that makes the book good.

EZRA: Humanity! What bullshit!
(*out*) I stilled the air with that one.
What you're calling 'humanity' is merely your minuscule and highly improbable love story, which you've used to dress up your suspect 'political positions' and 'social mores of the

time' – none of which have anything to do with the actual mind or behaviour of –

WELLINGTON: Now, wait a second –

NEWBERRY: You don't think Carbuncle could've fallen for a black woman.

EZRA: No, I ... sure, he could.
(*to Carbuncle*) Couldn't you?

CARBUNCLE: Yes, of course. My parents, however, would not have been impressed.

NEWBERRY: He exoticizes black women, but I gave him complexity. He appreciates Selma Thomas's writing. He falls in love with her, despite his misconceived notions of race.

CARBUNCLE: My goodness. That's rather beautiful. I think I could do that, yes.

EZRA: Borrowing Gordias Carbuncle or Ernest Hemingway or any other famous writer is an act of literary bloodsucking. It's claiming authorship over what a genius thinks. And that's not ethical!

NEWBERRY: I thought you said he didn't believe in genius.

EZRA: He didn't.

NEWBERRY: Right.
(*She laughs.*) Look at you. Been hoarding his great book. All to yourself. Poring over it every night like some devout

Talmud scholar. As if his words belonged to you and you alone.

EZRA: (*to Wellington*) I can't endorse her stupid book.

CARBUNCLE: Vivian!

EZRA: And I won't do readings or panels or anything with her!

NEWBERRY: Fine with me.

EZRA: Her Carbuncle's wrong. All wrong. In fact, I don't see how you can publish such an inaccurate work.

WELLINGTON: It's historical fiction, not biography.

EZRA: It makes me question your qualifications for handling *Eternal Hydra*.

WELLINGTON: Oh, Christ ...

CARBUNCLE: Are you insane?

EZRA: I might have to reconsider this deal.

WELLINGTON: Okay, wait, slow down. Just take a moment to calm down ...
(*He looks back and forth between Newberry and Ezra.*) What do you say we open the box?

NEWBERRY: What?

(*Wellington starts to open the box.*)

WELLINGTON: Gwendolyn Jackson's papers.

CARBUNCLE: He's already agreed!

EZRA: But the principle, Gordias.

WELLINGTON: Musty old thing …

CARBUNCLE: You can't just let it go!

EZRA: I'm protecting you! Can't you see that?

(*Wellington opens the box and looks inside.*)

WELLINGTON: Magazines. Parisian newspapers.

NEWBERRY: I'll bet some of those are quite valuable.

CARBUNCLE: Six years of work! All of it, down the drain! Why?
Because you don't like this Newberry woman's book?

EZRA: It's character assault. She's flushing your good name down
the drain with that depiction.

CARBUNCLE: That's ridiculous!

EZRA: Mr. Wellington.

(*Wellington looks up, papers in hand.*)

I have something I need to say. Your father started this firm with the loftiest of ideals. His pure love of literature. Since inception, Wellington and Company has been synonymous with integrity, honesty and quality. Am I wrong?

WELLINGTON: No.

EZRA: Unfortunately, as I see it, if you expect to maintain this firm's reputation, you can't have it both ways. You can either publish *Eternal Hydra* or Miss Newberry's novel. But not both.

WELLINGTON: You're not serious.

EZRA: I am absolutely serious, Mr. Wellington. You must choose the greater book.

WELLINGTON: All right. I choose hers.

CARBUNCLE: No! Vivian!

EZRA: *Eternal Hydra* is a masterpiece.

WELLINGTON: Yes, but is it any good? Or is it only 'great'? Do you like reading it, or does it feel like a chore? Is it emotionally moving, or just some rarified intellectual exercise?

EZRA: It moves me.

WELLINGTON: When I read Pauline's latest, I couldn't hold back the tears. I'll be honest with you. I'm not that interested in novels that want to be secular bibles. Books that turn reading into a quasi-religious act. My father was a visionary, yes.

His integrity suited his time and place. Well, I have integrity too. A novel has be pleasurable, Vivian, or else it's just not worth remembering.

EZRA: I see.

WELLINGTON: I'm very proud to publish the writers I believe in.

(*Ezra hugs the book, dejected.*)

Looks like you're going to crush that thing.

(*Ezra releases her grip.*)

I shouldn't have to choose. I hope you'll reconsider.

(*Ezra looks to Carbuncle, then back at Wellington. She shakes her head, clutching the manuscript.*)

EZRA: I'm sorry.

WELLINGTON: So am I.

(*Newberry, who has been looking through the box, removing various magazines and journals, now removes a diary.*)

NEWBERRY: What's this?

WELLINGTON: Looks like a diary.

CARBUNCLE: We should leave.

(*Wellington takes the diary.*)

EZRA: Gwendolyn Jackson's?

WELLINGTON: I don't think so.

CARBUNCLE: Right now!

EZRA: Whose?

WELLINGTON: (*reading*) June 14th, 1936. Woke up dreadful drunk and quickly poured myself a drink. Saw my own reflection and couldn't help but mutter *cripes*. Carbuncle! Ha! I've grown so fat and old.

NEWBERRY: It's his.

CARBUNCLE: We're done here. Let's visit Martin Warwick at Agamemnon Press.

EZRA: Is it really?

(*Wellington closes the diary and holds it up.*)

WELLINGTON: Would you like to read it, Vivian?

EZRA: Oh. Yes. Thank you.

(*Ezra reaches for the diary. Wellington holds it away.*)

WELLINGTON: Give me the book.

EZRA: (*out*) I had to do it.

(*Ezra hands Wellington the manuscript. He hands her the diary. She holds it tight.*)

WELLINGTON: I'll do a great job with *Eternal Hydra*.

NEWBERRY: (*to Ezra*) Aren't you going to look at it?

EZRA: Later, not here ...

WELLINGTON: You've made the right decision.

EZRA: Yes, well, I hope.

(*They shake hands.*)

WELLINGTON: Leave your address with Jenna outside, you'll get a preliminary contract in the mail. Come back in a couple weeks, we'll hammer out details.

EZRA: (*out*) I stood there for a moment, grinning stupidly. In disbelief.

(*Wellington looks at his watch.*)

WELLINGTON: Now, Pauline and I have some other business, if you don't mind.

EZRA: Yes, of course.

CARBUNCLE: Vivian, take that diary and throw it straight into the Hudson!

EZRA: (*out*) Suddenly, I didn't feel so well. And I couldn't bring myself to leave. So I turned to Pauline Newberry.
Your novel sounds wonderful. Despite my issues. I'm sure it'll be very successful.

NEWBERRY: I look forward to *Eternal Hydra*.

EZRA: I hope you enjoy it.

NEWBERRY: No doubt I will.

(*Ezra turns to Carbuncle. Carbuncle bows to Newberry.*)

CARBUNCLE: Goodbye, Miss Newberry. Congratulations on your wonderful accomplishment. And thank you for your complex portrayal of me.

EZRA: (*out*) I suddenly felt so alone.

(*Ezra and Carbuncle leave Wellington's office and stand alone.*)

(*out*) A huge letdown in the hallway.
We did it.

CARBUNCLE: You're upset.

EZRA: I was rash and mean and stupid.

CARBUNCLE: That's not true.

EZRA: Your diary.

CARBUNCLE: Don't read it.

EZRA: I have to.

CARBUNCLE: No, you don't.

EZRA: Even if you hate me.

CARBUNCLE: I could never hate you. After what you've done for me?

EZRA: Yes, you could.

CARBUNCLE: My sweet Juno.

EZRA: (*out*) He took my hand and gazed into my eyes.

CARBUNCLE: May I speak with hyperbole in order to make my point? In the history of written communication – for me personally – there are several key moments that stand out as highlights. Would you like to hear them?

EZRA: Okay.

CARBUNCLE: First. Jean-François Champollion deciphering the famed Rosetta Stone, cracking open the mystery of Egyptian hieroglyphics, unveiling the religion, culture and history of our planet's great ancient civilization ... that to me was a moment. Second. When a couple of English actors, no doubt quite unwashed, decided to gather together the plays of their moderately well-known peer William Shakespeare in order to publish a first folio of his theatrical work … that to me was a moment. And third, when a young scribe named Ezra, returning to Jerusalem from exile in Babylon, decided to redact and reinstate his people's holy text, thereby commencing the codification of what we now know as the Bible … that to me was a moment. You, Vivian, in this office here today, have just provided me with another.

EZRA: I have?

CARBUNCLE: You have.

(*Ezra laughs, thrilled.*)

EZRA: My Gordias.

CARBUNCLE: My Vivian. Throw away that diary.

Act Two

Scene One

(*Ezra stands alone. She opens the diary and reads.*)

EZRA: (*reading*) June 14th, 1936 ...

(*The scene has shifted to Gordias Carbuncle's Parisian apartment, 1936. A mess. There is a stand-up full-length mirror, centrally located. Clothes, papers, bits of food. Parts of Carbuncle's signature suit are scattered: his jacket on a chair, vest on the floor, a shoe under the table, etc. Ezra continues to read.*)

(*reading*) Woke up dreadful drunk and quickly poured myself a drink. Saw my own reflection. Couldn't help but mutter *cripes*. Carbuncle! Ha! I've grown so fat and old.

(*She turns and watches the scene. Carbuncle enters, hungover. He is wearing an undershirt, the pants from his suit and one shoe. He yawns, pours himself a drink. He staggers over to the mirror and looks at himself.*)

CARBUNCLE: Cripes ...
   (*He turns away in disgust. He looks again in the mirror.*)
Carbuncle! Ha!
   (*He turns away.*) Fat and old.

EZRA: (*reading*) Another laborious day dressing the corpse of Gordias.

(*Carbuncle looks around his apartment, finds his shirt.*)

51

CARBUNCLE: Shirt.

(*He smells it, puts it on.*) Sloppy, shabby, shitty shirt.

(*He chuckles, buttons it up and tucks it in. He looks in the mirror.*) Still recognizable. A demi-Carbuncle in his sloppy, shabby, shitty shirt!

(*He laughs.*) You pathetic, drunken Jew.

(*He turns away disgusted and continues to search the apartment. He finds his vest and his belt. He puts on the vest.*) Suck in your corpulence, pig.

(*He sucks in his gut, puts on his belt. Pats his belly. He finds his tie, goes to the mirror and ties it.*) Bit better. Over, under, hoppity-hop … little rabbit in the hole.

(*He chuckles. He turns to the side, pats his bum.*) All tucked in. Well, then, Carbuncle. Least you've got a tight tush for a genius over forty.

(*He smooths his hair, looks in the mirror, then looks around the room.*) Jacket.

(*He puts on his jacket.*) Kerchief.

(*He finds a handkerchief and shakes it out. It's covered with crumbs.*) Disgusting.

(*He tucks it in his jacket. He looks in the mirror and smiles. He primps and composes himself.*) Gordias Carbuncle, there you are!

(*He bows to the mirror, much more dignified.*) Sir, the pleasure's all mine.

(*Upon bowing, he notices that he's missing a shoe.*) Where's your goddamn shoe, gimp?

(*He finds the shoe, puts it on, returns to the mirror.*) There. Carbuncle, composed.

(*Carbuncle prepares himself for a visitor. He faces forward and calls out.*) Gwendolyn Jackson, entrez-vous!

(*The actor playing Ezra joins the scene, entering as Gwendolyn Jackson. She is carrying a stack of books and papers.*)

JACKSON: I believe that's all.

CARBUNCLE: Excellent!

(*Jackson puts the books down and rifles through her papers, making stacks.*)

JACKSON: Let's see ... here's information on the invasion and occupation of New Orleans, 1862. The policies of General Butler, Governor Wells, Confederate resistance, et cetera ... here's Freedman's Bureau and Loyal League information, plus migration patterns after emancipation ... here's suffrage, Black Codes, Knights of the White Camellia ... and here ... the large pile's on the New Orleans Riot of 1866, including maps of the city, newspaper articles and direct testimony from Henry Warmoth, as requested. It took me a week to locate.

CARBUNCLE: A week!

JACKSON: I do agree, Gordias, it's a very exciting period. Great potential for an extraordinary chapter. Oh! And I've written a small report.
　　(*She grabs a piece of paper.*) An overview. Main points, brief analysis, most dramatic events. Should be everything you need. A month's work. Take a look ...

CARBUNCLE: My sweet Gwendolyn ...

(*He approaches, Jackson backs away.*)

JACKSON: While you can. Because I'm going to burn it, you degenerate. You'll never see a sentence.

CARBUNCLE: Oh dear.

JACKSON: I'm neither your lackey nor your slave.

CARBUNCLE: I know that.

JACKSON: I'm a scholar of the highest order!

CARBUNCLE: Why do you think I've asked your help?

JACKSON: You ignore me. You could telephone.

CARBUNCLE: You're right. I could and should and will do so in the future.

JACKSON: You can't treat me this way! After everything I've done! I have my dignity, sir!

(*Carbuncle approaches Jackson, slowly.*)

CARBUNCLE: My Gwendolyn, I know you're upset, but don't let's resort to dignity.

JACKSON: I have my pride.

CARBUNCLE: Dignity's such a burden! Save it for the austerity of the public realm. True human lives have nothing to do with it.

JACKSON: Don't you get clever with me, Gordias.

CARBUNCLE: You must rid yourself of your dignity as I have rid myself of mine.

(*He stands close to her.*) Dignity and pleasure are eternal foes.

JACKSON: You haven't called me in three weeks.

CARBUNCLE: I am sorry. I've been drinking and working and sleeping late. I've completely lost track of myself. Look at me. I'm a mess.

JACKSON: Yes, you are. You're a vile, putrid gorilla, squatting in your own filth! Making meals of your excrement!

CARBUNCLE: Well, it may not be your intention, but you're beginning to make me horny ...

JACKSON: Stop it!
(*She pulls away from him.*) I will not be used by you.

CARBUNCLE: I'm not trying to –

JACKSON: You need me. I've given you hours and hours of research. Seventy-one chapters thus far, now the source material for seventy-two!

CARBUNCLE: Now, let's be fair. You've helped with twenty-five at most.

JACKSON: More!

CARBUNCLE: Thirty-five.

JACKSON: Forty! It's not the point! You are indebted to me, Gordias!

CARBUNCLE: I don't deny it.

JACKSON: It's my book as well!

CARBUNCLE: All right. Calm down.

JACKSON: I will not!

CARBUNCLE: Have a seat.

JACKSON: No!

CARBUNCLE: Well, what do you want from me then? Compensation? A little star from teacher to put in your notebook? You've always known what kind of work this would be.

(*Jackson sits.*)

Would you like a drink?

JACKSON: No.

CARBUNCLE: I think I will.

(*Carbuncle pours himself a drink and sits.*)

JACKSON: As a matter of fact, I would like compensation, yes. That's exactly what I would like.

CARBUNCLE: You have something particular in mind?

JACKSON: Well, I thought I could, perhaps ... write an introduction. A glowing preface to help acquaint the reader.

CARBUNCLE: No!

JACKSON: It's a very common practice. I'm extremely qualified.

CARBUNCLE: Readers can make their own acquaintance. Let the author precede the scholar! Introductions are pure thievery.

JACKSON: That's absurd.

CARBUNCLE: Not at all. I'll give you a rhetorical example. Let's suppose I'm an American – god forbid – either religious or drunk or both, and I've written an encyclopedic novel about a whaling vessel. There's an insane sea captain, whom I shall christen Ahab, leading a makeshift band of whalers – hunting, harpooning, feasting blubber on the sea. They embark upon a quasi-mystical journey to capture a giant white whale that I shall call Richard, or Dick, for short. Suppose this novel is very good. Now suppose you're an upstart scholar. You fancy yourself both a mariner and a mystic, and you've written an introduction to my novel. A very common practice, as you say. In your introduction, you have generously plotted out the entire voyage of my fictional ship – which I shall call the Pequod. You include a detailed map indicating the Pequod's travels, right up to the climactic moment when the whaler gloriously sinks. The novel's end. Moreover, you thoroughly discuss the meaning of all these events. Which means, of course, that when average readers pick up my great opus, peruse your benevolent introduction and glance at your remarkably telling map, they read my novel with complete knowledge of plot, theme, structure, tone, et cetera. The scholar who writes such an introduction is a thief. My novel merely fills in blanks from her introduction. It's a footnote to

her map. It's now her book, really, the scholar's, no longer
mine, the author's.

JACKSON: Yes, of course. That's right.

(*Carbuncle grabs a copy of* Moby Dick.)

CARBUNCLE: The situation is not hypothetical. I present you
with material evidence.
    (*He gives her the novel.*) Regard the introductory map. The
little picture of the Pequod sinking into the Pacific. Were I
Melville, I would murder.

JACKSON: I would be cautious of such errors.

CARBUNCLE: I don't want an introduction.

JACKSON: I want my rightful place. You owe me my rightful
place. I won't be left behind. I see what you do. Spouting
your charming anecdotes about ancient India and China, as if
you've discovered them yourself. The stories I found for you,
translated directly into your book. And with me standing
there beside you like some meek secretary. Why is that,
Gordias? You tell people at parties – last week even – that
you're spending all your time alone. Nothing of my research,
ever. I hear you. You're a beautiful writer. I don't dispute it. But
I want my rightful place.

CARBUNCLE: Yes.

JACKSON: It's only fair.

(Carbuncle pours himself a large drink.)

I don't like your act. You think I can't see through it? Your pompous, pretentious manner. The way you sally up to us all. The little game of your seduction. 'Dignity and pleasure, my Gwendolyn, they are forever eternal foes.' That isn't you, Gordias. That's just some clever beast.

(Carbuncle drinks. He quickly pours himself another.)

How is it I can love you so deeply, but have no idea who you are?

(He drinks again, despondent.)

What?

CARBUNCLE: Let's burn it.

JACKSON: Oh God … not again …

CARBUNCLE: The whole thing. Come, let's do it …

(She comes to him, holds him.)

JACKSON: You strange man …

CARBUNCLE: Rid the world of Gordias Carbuncle.

JACKSON: You've written a work of genius. Can't you see that? Doesn't matter if anyone else on this planet ever gets to read it. I know what it is. You can't burn it. I won't let you. I'll steal it from you and lock it away and read it a thousand times myself. Never let it out of my sight, ever in this life, my dear sweet man.

CARBUNCLE: There will be no introduction. No commentary.

JACKSON: Gordias …

CARBUNCLE: You'll get no credit. You can have nothing. I offer you absolutely nothing.

JACKSON: I don't need credit. You've already offered me everything.

(*She tries to kiss him. Carbuncle is cold. Jackson pulls away.*)

Right. Of course.

(*She leaves. Carbuncle goes to mirror and stares at himself.*)

CARBUNCLE: One can't but wonder. Should Carbuncle love her? Love? Her? Is this creature, Gordias Carbuncle, capable of such emotion? I don't think he is. That does not seem to be a significant part of his character. I think he's a cold fish.
  (*He studies himself in the mirror closely.*) I know that face. I distinctly recognize that face. But the voice … and the clothes. Are you that Dublin Jewish boy who lived on St. Kevin's Parade? The one who never ate pig? Not possible. Not you. Now, I see you devour prosciutto.
  (*He postures in the mirror.*) How good of you to eat prosciutto.

(*Ezra closes the diary, distraught.*)

Scene Two

(*Newberry speaks in direct audience address.*)

NEWBERRY: (*out*) Chapter seventy-two, I said. New Orleans, Louisiana, 1866.

(*Sitting behind her desk, Ezra withdraws a manuscript. She opens it carefully.*)

NEWBERRY: (*out*) I was visiting Professor Ezra at Brown University. A beautiful office: slanted ceilings, original mouldings, sleek posters from the Weimar Republic. Top floor of an old colonial house on George St., Providence.

EZRA: (*searching*) Let me see ...

NEWBERRY: (*out*) It was like a small library. Books in every corner, stashed on every shelf. Scholarly works, academic journals, literary editions. The place was packed. One additional stack of books and she wouldn't be able to reach the door.

EZRA: Here, take a look.

(*Ezra hands the manuscript to Newberry.*)

NEWBERRY: (*out*) It was a year after we'd met. I'd just read *Eternal Hydra*, still in galleys, a month away from being published. I'd never read anything like it. An astonishing experience. Especially when I hit chapter seventy-two.

(*Newberry studies the manuscript.*)

EZRA: The notes and rewrites are all his.

NEWBERRY: But the main text is typed.

EZRA: The first draft's no longer extant.

NEWBERRY: So you don't know who actually wrote it.

EZRA: Gordias Carbuncle did.

NEWBERRY: I'm not so sure.
(*She returns the manuscript. She withdraws papers from her briefcase.*) When I was researching Selma Thomas, I found her stories and early works. I unearthed some obscure bits that –

EZRA: Doesn't matter.

NEWBERRY: Well, at least take a look.
(*Newberry hands her the papers.*) (*out*) Some fragments of the chapter in Selma Thomas's handwriting. Dating from the mid-1920s, when she lived in New Orleans. Long before Paris, or Gordias Carbuncle.

(*Ezra rifles through the pages.*)

You see? Many of the key details are there. Cobblers' terms and tools. Mechanics' Institute and the riot of July 30th. There's even mention of a magnolia dress and a soldier named Lawful.

(*Ezra checks.*)

EZRA: I'm sorry … could you, please …

NEWBERRY: Naturally, this presents a serious problem for publication.

EZRA: Could you excuse me for a moment?

(*Ezra stands and goes to the window.*)

NEWBERRY: (*out*) She had to take a minute at the window by herself.

EZRA: (*quietly*) I will, I will …
(*turning back*) If you think for one second this will stop Wellington –

NEWBERRY: Whoa, hang on …

EZRA: Because it absolutely won't.

NEWBERRY: I find these similarities troubling.

EZRA: I'm not surprised. Given your particular bias.

NEWBERRY: (*out*) I could see this was not going to be as easy as I'd hoped.

EZRA: Your novel last year already set him up as a nightmare!

NEWBERRY: Look, Vivian, I don't hate him.

EZRA: Well, you don't exactly love him! I mean, how could you? I'm not saying you have to, either, only … you see some abusive demagogue in his shoes.

NEWBERRY: I don't know what he is.

EZRA: Well, I think you should try to see him clearly before you go around calling him a thief!

NEWBERRY: You're right, I should. So help me.
(*out*) My suggestion startled her.

EZRA: All right. Carbuncle in the 1930s was scared and desperate. Facing the grim reality of Nazi Germany. Not to mention his own mortality. He was an outsider, himself. A Jew in fascist Europe. You have to understand the full pressure of anti-Semitism at that time. You have to try to picture the man as he was, in his own time and place …

NEWBERRY: (*out*) I should've realized right away that Vivian wouldn't help me. It wasn't a question of proof. It was a question of love.

EZRA: Try to imagine him completely. His accent. His appearance.

NEWBERRY: Okay …

(*Carbuncle appears.*)

How would he defend himself?

EZRA: Well, he'd clearly say:

CARBUNCLE: I wrote every damn word of that book!

NEWBERRY: And if I told him what I found?

EZRA: Well, I'm sure he'd still say:

CARBUNCLE: I wrote every damn word of that book!

NEWBERRY: (*out*) Like I said. Not easy.

I distinctly remember a note he wrote to his cousin at Trinity that paints a very different picture of this matter. Have you got his letters?

(*out*) Reluctantly, Vivian grabbed a dog-eared copy of Gordias Carbuncle's correspondence.

(*Ezra hands her the book. Newberry finds the page and Carbuncle appears.*)

Here. August 18th, 1929. Dear Daniel –

CARBUNCLE: Thank you for the grim but not altogether unexpected news about my unfortunate mother. I'm really not surprised this happened to her, given her foul mouth and reckless drinking. I trust she's comfortable now, and as happy as she could be, considering her maudlin tendencies.

EZRA: You don't have to read the whole thing.

NEWBERRY: Okay. Here …

CARBUNCLE: In answer to your question, I've heard that complaint before. Always thought it absurd. Every author uses source material. For the life of me, I cannot comprehend this puritanical obsession with authorship!

EZRA: Genius is dead. That's all he means.

CARBUNCLE: Those obsessed with pure authorship are fighting a losing battle. Words exist in free circulation. Ideas, plots, phrases. All literature's a mere phyllo dough of theft. There has never been such a thing as an original idea, an original source. There's no master text.

EZRA: That's hardly incriminating. He's outlining the nature of modernist composition as he sees it.

NEWBERRY: Sounds to me like a good excuse to steal a black woman's story.

EZRA: You're twisting his words for your own ends!

NEWBERRY: I read the letter as written!

EZRA: I'm sorry, Pauline. I … I'm going to have to ask you to leave.

(*Carbuncle exits.*)

NEWBERRY: Vivian …

EZRA: I have other appointments.

NEWBERRY: Do you really want a battle? You want lawyers involved? (*Pause.*) Look, there's clearly enough information to call Carbuncle's authorship into question. So why don't you help me figure out what part is hers and what is his. I'm sure we can solve this thing together. And when it's resolved, you can add some footnotes, recontextualize the chapter, and let Selma be rightfully served.

EZRA: It's quite possible they worked from the same source material.

NEWBERRY: She had no money. No respect at home. Hardly more in Paris. A black woman in the 1930s. No possibilities for acclaim. She wrote a story about the riot of New Orleans and never got to publish it. You really want to keep that injustice going?

EZRA: No. But I …

NEWBERRY: You what?

EZRA: I can't.

(*Pause.*)

NEWBERRY: There's more. I'm editing a collection of Selma Thomas's stories. Wellington's going to publish it. There's growing interest in her work.

EZRA: Because of your novel?

NEWBERRY: I'd like to include this chapter. I want to name Selma Thomas as the co-author.

EZRA: You would never!

NEWBERRY: I'm going to set this record straight.

EZRA: Oh, yes, I can see you're hell-bent on doing that! And you clearly don't mind reducing what was I'm sure a complex, very complex, very complicated and complex situation into some blunt headline! *Gordias Carbuncle: A Thief! Irish Writer: A Good-for-Nothing Racist!* I won't have Carbuncle disdained, abused, shat on, dragged through the mud like Bertolt Brecht.

NEWBERRY: Whatever happened to Carbuncle's diary? Randall told me you never returned it. Asked you five or six times, but you always told him there was more work.

EZRA: There was. There always is.

NEWBERRY: What exactly did he write?

(*Ezra turns away.*)

If you know something –

EZRA: Nothing.

NEWBERRY: If you –

EZRA: I told you nothing.

NEWBERRY: That would have very serious consequences for your academic career.

EZRA: Yes. Well, yes.

(*Pause.*)

NEWBERRY: They slept together.

EZRA: Oh, how preposterous!

NEWBERRY: They were in love with each other.

EZRA: His life is not your stupid novel!

NEWBERRY: I had a feeling all along.

EZRA: Their relationship was entirely professional!

NEWBERRY: You know that for a fact?

(*Pause. Ezra withdraws the diary from her desk, finds the right page and hands it to Newberry.*)

EZRA: Here.

NEWBERRY: (*reading*) June 15th, 1936. The American writer Selma Thomas stopped by my flat today, at my own request.

(*Carbuncle's world returns.*)

CARBUNCLE: Entrez-vous, entrez-vous!

(*The actor playing Newberry enters as Selma Thomas. She is obviously poor.*)

Please, don't be sheepish. Have a drink.

(*Thomas steps into the room.*)

THOMAS: We've met before.

CARBUNCLE: I remember. Two years ago.

THOMAS: I got a note this morning from Paulette Nardal.

CARBUNCLE: Yes, I sent it.

THOMAS: I've read your stories, Mr. Carbuncle.

CARBUNCLE: Oh, good lord. Call me Gordias.

THOMAS: They're very good.

CARBUNCLE: You're too kind. Those stories are mere kindling for the fire roaring within me now.

THOMAS: A new novel? I've heard rumours about it.

CARBUNCLE: Thank you for coming.

THOMAS: How do you know Paulette?

CARBUNCLE: On occasion, I used to attend the salon she ran with Monsieur Achille on Rue Geoffroy-Saint-Hilaire.

THOMAS: You did?

CARBUNCLE: You're surprised.

THOMAS: I never saw a white man there.

CARBUNCLE: I stuck out, to put it mildly. Like an infected white boil.
    (*He smiles.*) I only visited twice. A fantastic idea, really.

THOMAS: I always thought so.

CARBUNCLE: A completely Parisian salon with the best in French Negro minds!

THOMAS: So you have an interest in Negro art?

CARBUNCLE: Oh, very much so. The discussions, there. Such brilliance. During my final attendance, there was a young student from the colonies of West Africa. Quiet man. Perfect French. Spoke some measured words about the international unity of the Negro experience. Across cultures and languages. He claimed there's a cohesive artistic essence buried within the Negro race.

THOMAS: You mean Monsieur Senghor. Every human race has its own distinct culture and thought. Neither better, nor worse, just different.

CARBUNCLE: You know him?

THOMAS: We've met.

CARBUNCLE: You agree with him?

THOMAS: I don't know.

CARBUNCLE: I think he's making a terrible mistake. Each race a different head! Each type of human thinking differently from the others ... African, German, Toltec or Tibetan ... it's missing the point.

THOMAS: How so?

CARBUNCLE: We're humans. We're all the same! We're not so different because of race. One dreams that our brains define us. No. Fallacy. We are material objects, us humans, meaty things that ooze. We share guts, liver, lungs and spleen … viscera and gore define us. Humans, collectively, are one creature. We are the multi-headed hydra of classical fame – eternal, ugly, mythic – and though each of our 'unique' hydra heads may hold different thoughts, each with its own history and bitter will towards independence, we have just one body. The same coarse blood, the same molecules, the same stomach and heart and instinct within. Is it such wonder that we hate one another?

THOMAS: I'll be sure to edify Monsieur Senghor.

(*Carbuncle laughs.*)

CARBUNCLE: That's not a terrible idea …

THOMAS: The last thing Léopold Senghor needs right now is another white man's theory.

CARBUNCLE: I'm sure you're right. You're a very lovely woman.

THOMAS: The classical hydra wasn't eternal. It was killed by Hercules.

CARBUNCLE: Was it?

THOMAS: Your analogy's simplistic.

CARBUNCLE: That depends upon the identity of Hercules. In my analogy.

(*Carbuncle is smiling. Thomas smiles.*)

THOMAS: Hercules. Let me see … a hero with the mythic task of conquering all humanity. The superman who captures each of the hydra's heads. And how does he do it, this capturing? I think he does it in writing …

CARBUNCLE: My dear Selma, would you care for a glass of Tullamore Dew?

THOMAS: I would, thank you.

(*Carbuncle pours two glasses. Thomas takes one. They watch each other and drink.*)

Are you trying to get me drunk?

CARBUNCLE: Yes.

(*They drink.*)

The drunker the better, in fact.

THOMAS: I hate to disappoint, but I won't be sleeping with you tonight.

CARBUNCLE: Oh dear. You mean to tell me you're not my personal Josephine?

THOMAS: No banana skirts in my closet.

CARBUNCLE: No leopards and cheetahs for pets?

THOMAS: Jazz doesn't make me horny.

CARBUNCLE: What does, then?

THOMAS: Gregorian chants.

(*Carbuncle roars with laughter.*)

CARBUNCLE: I'm trying to get you drunk so that you'll show me one of your stories.

THOMAS: Really?

CARBUNCLE: I've heard it's the only way. Your reticence has acquired a certain fame.

THOMAS: Which story?

CARBUNCLE: I don't know the title. A first-person narrative, told from the perspective of a Louisiana woman just after the American Civil War. The riot of New Orleans, something of the sort.

THOMAS: I've never shown that story to anyone.

CARBUNCLE: I'm sure it's excellent.

THOMAS: Where'd you hear about it?

CARBUNCLE: From Paulette. She was considering one of your stories for publication in *La Revue du monde noir* several years ago.

THOMAS: That's right. Before it folded.

CARBUNCLE: Very unfortunate.

THOMAS: A disaster, actually. It would've meant forty francs.

CARBUNCLE: Too bad. Another drink?

(*Carbuncle pours her another. Thomas drinks.*)

May I see your story?

THOMAS: Tell me something, Gordias.

CARBUNCLE: Anything, Selma.

THOMAS: What's your name?

(*Carbuncle drinks.*)

CARBUNCLE: I am Gordias Carbuncle. Author of *Eternal Hydra*.

THOMAS: *Eternal Hydra* isn't finished.

CARBUNCLE: It's how I'll be known in the future. The book is sure to make me famous.

THOMAS: Gordias Carbuncle ... King Gordias, right?

CARBUNCLE: Mythical king of Phrygia. Founder of the city Gordium.

THOMAS: The man behind the Gordian knot.

CARBUNCLE: I believe that's correct. Study mythology, do you?

THOMAS: A little. Carbuncle. That's a pimple. Worse, even. A flaming, putrid, malignant boil.

CARBUNCLE: One definition. There's another. Resplendent jewel. A ruby or a sapphire. With a brilliance so mythic it emits its glowing light even in the absolute dark.

THOMAS: And you're which one, jewel or boil?

(*They share a smile.*)

I want to know your real name.

CARBUNCLE: I told you. Gordias Carbuncle.

THOMAS: And before you were Gordias Carbuncle you were … ?

CARBUNCLE: Some faceless Irish Jew.

THOMAS: Named?

CARBUNCLE: Have another drink.
(*He takes her glass and pours her another drink.*) Names are words. They can be rewritten, like all words.

THOMAS: Unlike, say, the colour of your skin?

CARBUNCLE: Yes.

THOMAS: Which is a bit less susceptible to erasing and rewriting.

CARBUNCLE: Will you show me your story or not?

THOMAS: Not.

CARBUNCLE: I'll give you money for it. As a matter of fact, I'll offer you one hundred American dollars if you sell me your story and make no further claims on its authorship.

THOMAS: A hundred bucks?

CARBUNCLE: Yes. You can go back to America. You can buy yourself several months. Write other stories, better stories. You clearly have the talent, if only you had the time. Time is what you crave. Isn't it?

THOMAS: Where'd you get a hundred bucks to blow on buying stories?

CARBUNCLE: From a rich friend. Is it a deal? Selma, why are you still in Paris? All of the others have left. Europe is no place today for a woman with an American passport. With Spain escalating. Germans mixed up in it. I'm certain it won't be long before we're all again at war. You should be back home.

THOMAS: I don't have the money to get home.

CARBUNCLE: But I am presently saying I will give you one hundred American dollars. Your glass is looking empty.

(*Thomas hands it to Carbuncle. He fills it.*)

THOMAS: What would you do with my story?

CARBUNCLE: Use it in my novel. Extensively rewritten, of course. As the basis for one of my hundred chapters.

THOMAS: You don't have a problem with that?

CARBUNCLE: Why should I have a problem with that?

THOMAS: Because you didn't write it.

CARBUNCLE: These days writing is a very small part of being an author. You can have your money today.

THOMAS: You haven't seen my story.

CARBUNCLE: I'm certain I'll find something of use.

THOMAS: I don't have it with me.

CARBUNCLE: Send it to me before you leave.

THOMAS: Goddamn you.

CARBUNCLE: I'm sorry?

(*Thomas holds out her hand.*)

THOMAS: Give me the money.

(*Carbuncle takes out his wallet and removes five crisp American twenty-dollar bills. He holds them up.*)

They look very fresh.

CARBUNCLE: For some reason, the American Express office over on Rue Scribe seems to have the freshest currency.
(*Carbuncle hands her the money.*) You have my address?

THOMAS: I do. You're smart. The editor and author, a single man. Why put yourself in another's shoes when you can buy those shoes from off her feet?

CARBUNCLE: It's just, I'm very ambitious. And I'm aware of my own limitations.

THOMAS: I understand. I spent a long time writing the story you just bought. Almost a year. Writing, erasing, rewriting. Trying to find the voice of a former slave. My grandmother was a slave in Louisiana. Freed when General Butler took New Orleans in the summer of '62. Ditched the fields and made her way to the Crescent City. Lived through the riot of 1866. You know about it?

CARBUNCLE: I'm vaguely familiar with the event.

THOMAS: You know what she wrote about that day? Nothing. No opinions for posterity. She never learned to write. Never had a chance to put her views to paper.

CARBUNCLE: Yes.

THOMAS: I took a year of my life. Gave her the public voice she was never able to claim for herself.

CARBUNCLE: That's very admirable. I mean that quite sincerely.

THOMAS: Is it admirable? I'm not so sure. I'm no more authentic than you. I'm not my grandmother, never been a slave, I hope never to be. I wasn't around New Orleans, 1866. I faked it. That's all.

CARBUNCLE: It seems forgery's the nature of our profession.

THOMAS: Yes, it does.

CARBUNCLE: Tell me. Will you leave Paris immediately?

THOMAS: Most likely.

CARBUNCLE: I'll be sorry. I've enjoyed our conversation.

THOMAS: So have I.

CARBUNCLE: A pleasure to see you. A great pleasure.
    (*He stands and bows, slightly.*) Have a very safe trip home.

THOMAS: Thank you.

CARBUNCLE: Hope there are no storms on your passage.

THOMAS: Same with me.

CARBUNCLE: I hope the food is agreeable on the ship.

THOMAS: I'm sure it will be.

CARBUNCLE: Yes, I'm sure.

THOMAS: Aren't you the least bit ashamed?

CARBUNCLE: Aren't you?

(*Carbuncle's world disappears. Newberry opens the diary and leaves it onstage.*)

Act Three

(Wellington Jr. speaks Carbuncle's diary.)

WELLINGTON: *(out)* June 16th, 1936. Randall Wellington's in town and I arranged to meet with him.

(Carbuncle's world rises.)

CARBUNCLE: Entrez-vous, entrez-vous!

(The actor playing Wellington Jr. enters as Wellington Sr.)

WELLINGTON: Gordias Carbuncle!

CARBUNCLE: Mr. Wellington. How long are you in Paris?

WELLINGTON: Just two weeks. Place has changed.

CARBUNCLE: Considerably.

WELLINGTON: Where're all the party boys?

CARBUNCLE: Back in America and England, nursing their hangovers.

WELLINGTON: Too bad.

CARBUNCLE: How's Mrs. Wellington?

WELLINGTON: Don't know and don't care. Drink?

CARBUNCLE: Help yourself.

(*Wellington pours himself a drink.*)

WELLINGTON: You look good. Writing?

CARBUNCLE: Always.

WELLINGTON: Got your note at the hotel.

CARBUNCLE: Yes.

WELLINGTON: Finished the book?

(*Wellington drinks.*)

CARBUNCLE: I'm afraid not. Unfortunately, I have some financial concerns.

WELLINGTON: What is this crap?

CARBUNCLE: Excuse me?

WELLINGTON: The crap in the cup.

CARBUNCLE: That 'crap' is a thrice-distilled, all-barley Irish classic. My signature poison. Tullamore Dew.

WELLINGTON: It tastes like urine.

CARBUNCLE: You have some experience tasting urine?

WELLINGTON: You're a cultured man, Carbuncle. Get your hands on a good scotch. A White Horse or something.

CARBUNCLE: Unlike Americans, I detest the smell of smoked peat. I'm quite satisfied, thank you.

WELLINGTON: Suit yourself. So. Money.

CARBUNCLE: I have none of it.

WELLINGTON: Surprise, surprise.

CARBUNCLE: I've mismanaged a bit.

WELLINGTON: I'm sure.

CARBUNCLE: However, I'm seventy-one chapters into my novel, out of a projected one hundred. The present chapter's set in New Orleans. Writing proceeds splendidly.

WELLINGTON: Great.

CARBUNCLE: Only, each chapter requires a tremendous amount of research as it represents the voice of a character with unique perspective and knowledge. More research than I expected. It takes quite a lot of time. I need several more years to finish.

WELLINGTON: Years?

CARBUNCLE: Mr. Wellington, I can't do this without money. I spend most of my days and nights alone, working in my apartment. I have no time to prepare my supper and so I visit cafés.

I'll admit I drink to excess and that's a stress on my funds. But I work. How I work. It's simply a matter of time. Anything you give I'll repay with hundreds of wonderful pages.

WELLINGTON: Nice pitch.

CARBUNCLE: I'll finish my book. It will be a work of complete genius. Soon to become the feather in Wellington and Company's cap.

WELLINGTON: You sure about that?

CARBUNCLE: You've read my Moroccan stories. You know my talent.

WELLINGTON: Let's see a sample. So I know what I'm buying.

CARBUNCLE: I'm afraid I can't until it's finished.

WELLINGTON: So I take a total risk?

CARBUNCLE: You know me. My reputation. I am very uncomfortable with this part of my profession. Please, Randall. Write me a cheque.

WELLINGTON: Please?

CARBUNCLE: Yes, please.

(*Wellington stands and looks around.*)

WELLINGTON: Your place is a mess.

CARBUNCLE: I'm a sloppy bachelor. I haven't a maid.

(*Wellington looks at himself in the mirror.*)

WELLINGTON: The prerogative of genius, I guess.
(*He smooths his clothes, hair, etc.*) Once upon a time the men
who funded artists were revered. Kings and queens and dukes.
Cosmo de' Medici on the Florentine throne. The guys
Michelangelo bowed to. Haydn, Dante, Mozart.

CARBUNCLE: I have nothing but respect for you, Mr. Wellington.

WELLINGTON: They bowed to their patrons, those artists.

CARBUNCLE: Their patrons were royalty.

(*Wellington takes out a chequebook. He sits and writes a cheque.*)

WELLINGTON: Tell me again about this book I'm buying.

CARBUNCLE: It's called *Eternal Hydra*. There will be one hundred
separate voices, one hundred hydra heads. Each is a silenced
voice, drowned out by the roar of history – a samurai pining
for his son during the siege of Osaka Castle, a peasant pray-
ing in a stave church in Norway's civil wars, a trolley car oper-
ator with a winning sweepstakes ticket on the night shift in
sleepy Toronto. The protagonist is an interloper, a shape-
shifter. He's the victor of history. A pseudo-Herculean figure,
responsible for silencing the hundred voices, but also the one
who speaks for them. My intention is to create a complete
anti-myth for modernity. Rather than a demigod's heroism, we
find human weakness and compromise. Nothing will be

missing from my vision of humanity, except for God, of course, and His tedious arrogance. The book will be a moral triumph, a shimmering truth that reveals the fallacy of history.

WELLINGTON: (*chuckling*) That's romantic bullshit and you know it.

CARBUNCLE: No, it's not.

WELLINGTON: You're writing a book, Carbuncle. Like other books. Words are things. Your job is to make those things. You're a craftsman. A novel's not all that different from a chair, or a bar of soap, or a carburetor. If it works, people will use it. You're a factory.
(*He hands Carbuncle a cheque. Carbuncle accepts it.*) And I'm the means of production.

CARBUNCLE: I'm not a factory. I'm an artist.

WELLINGTON: Oh, Christ …
(*He pours himself a drink.*) You want one?

(*Carbuncle nods. Wellington pours him one.*)

You writers with your big-ballooning fictions in your heads …

(*They drink.*)

I love books. Reading 'em, owning 'em. Fill me with joy. Way more interesting than bars of soap. Not as profitable, but more interesting. And I like the guys who make books. Deluded fuckers, all of you. Running around Paris, drunk and randy, like a pack of ungodly priests, spinning quasi-religious fantasies around yourselves because you chip away at language instead of wood or steel –

CARBUNCLE: Or soap.

WELLINGTON: Because your raw material – language – is the same raw material used by Moses and the disciples. Writers. Hubris by the truckload. And never thinking your philosophies through. You all say there's no God. No God in the modern world of 1936, just a bunch of Nazis and Communists and Capitalists. But none of you modern writers seem to recognize that no God means no morality. I mean, really. You boast about the moral triumph of your work, but what are you basing that on, if not God? Your own divinity? No God means no divine preference of one thing over another. No absolute hierarchy of value. Period. Without morality, everything is equal: art, commerce, sewage. And that's just fine with me. Hell, I love art, but not because it's good for you. I like the hopelessly decadent, broken stories, written by people, not gods. My schnauzer's lower intestine has the same morality as the world's greatest novel!

CARBUNCLE: Ah, but you have a very fine schnauzer.

(*Wellington laughs.*)

I don't disagree with you, Randall.
    (*He drinks.*) You're quite gleeful without God.

WELLINGTON: I am. Good riddance! You know, you might be a better writer, Carbuncle, if you killed him off, as well.

CARBUNCLE: But you're fooling yourself. I don't think you've killed him off at all. In fact, I detect a strong scent of the old deity in your suit.

WELLINGTON: Oh yeah? How's that?

CARBUNCLE: Recall the covenant. Exodus 34:26. The Hebrew God demands the 'best of the first fruits of the ground,' which I should think means all material goods – grains, meats, what have you. God takes a piece of everything produced by his Israelite subjects for his own consumption. God likes to own things. The very first and best of things. Much like a factory owner. Correct? And, as the Gospel of John attests, words are God's possessions, too. 'In the beginning was the Word, and the Word was with God, and the Word was God.' Words are His products above all others. His very life. The most useful things of all. And more fun than a bar of soap for the truly ambitious collector.

(*Wellington laughs.*)

We are jealous creatures, aspiring divinities.

WELLINGTON: I like you, Carbuncle. Way more than my factory guys. They don't have your blasphemous aspiration. I'd rather spend an evening with you.

CARBUNCLE: Would you?

WELLINGTON: Certainly.

CARBUNCLE: You can't stay. I have no food.

WELLINGTON: Who says I want to eat?
(*Wellington stares at him.*) Gordias Carbuncle.

CARBUNCLE: Yes.

WELLINGTON: How'd you get that name like that?

(*Wellington touches Carbuncle.*)

CARBUNCLE: It's getting late, if you don't mind …

WELLINGTON: A Jew from Ireland. You know how ridiculous that is?

CARBUNCLE: Why do you think I left?

WELLINGTON: Pour me another drink.

(*Carbuncle pours Wellington a drink, which he downs quickly.*)

Ahh … (*He puts down the glass.*)
The money I paid you, you better be another Joyce.

(*He smiles and exits.*)

CARBUNCLE: I am nothing close.

(*Carbuncle stands and looks at himself in the mirror.*)

CARBUNCLE: Jacob Figatner …
You're a leech and a fraud. A drunk and a bore. They can see right through you. I'm sure they laugh at you behind your back,

tell stories at your expense. You're a thief and you've no talent. Look at you. Big ugly nose, fattening paunch. Losing your hair and you're stupid. You're self-obsessed. Shows in everything you say and everything you do or try to say or do and in everything you ever think. I think I hate you. Why am I stuck with you? You're loathsome. I long to abandon you in the gutters like some aborted fetus. You reek. You're pathetic, and ...

(*He stops himself, then quietly sings the first phrase from 'O Tannenbaum.'*) Ba dum da-da, da dum da-da, la-da-da-da da dum-da-da...

(*He pours himself a drink, drinks it fast, pours himself a drink and makes a toast to himself.*) To Gordias Carbuncle, artist, genius! Author of *Eternal Hydra*!

(*He drinks, then looks in the mirror. He begins to undress slowly, scattering his clothes.*) An aspiring divinity. Small god in the shallow heavens, hovering above *Eternal Hydra*'s pages. Brooding justice. Gazing down, with slight myopia, upon his created universe. The written words below. Declaiming with his grandeur: 'This is good, that's not so good.' Cruel judgment for phrases fashioned from his own pen. Crueler judgment, still, for the chapters crafted from stolen sources. Oh, there's morality, Mr. Wellington. Pure and fixed and true. The morality of Carbuncle's whim! The moral truth of his personal need and hunger! Inviolable code of law! Heh. Not a perfect world, no. Not a perfect god, this author. A bit too corpulent, for one. Quite flawed, all in all.

(*He pours a drink. Drinks, while looking at himself in the mirror.*) Nonetheless, I must confess, Carbuncle's universe is superior to Adolph Hitler's.

(*He returns to the table, pours himself another large drink.*) So goddamn drunk ...

(*He raises his glass.*) To me!

(*He drinks, puts down the glass.*) Whoever the hell that is.

(*Carbuncle's world disappears as he exits. Wellington Jr. is sitting at his desk in his office, reading the diary. Newberry and Ezra are in a meeting with him.*)

WELLINGTON: Hm.
(*out*) I said.

NEWBERRY: Not what you expected?

WELLINGTON: I don't know. Yes and no. To think my infallible father could be charmed and seduced. And Carbuncle! Incredible.
We'll have to delay *Eternal Hydra* by six months. Spring instead of fall. It'll cost a whack of money, but it's a newsworthy event. With the right press, I'll make up the loss in additional sales.
(*out*) But Pauline was already way ahead of me.

NEWBERRY: I think you should publish Carbuncle's diary the following season.

WELLINGTON: Interesting.

NEWBERRY: Maybe a similar cover. Tie the two together.

WELLINGTON: Vivian can rewrite the introduction. Acknowledge Carbuncle's theft, but also give an explanation. Then get to work editing the diary, to be published in the fall.
(*out*) Vivian just sat there, staring into her hands.
Hello?

EZRA: What? Oh. Yes. Fine.

WELLINGTON: When the monster superstores get their hands on this, with their famous writer T-shirts and shopping bags, we'll probably see sketches of Selma Thomas wearing a Gordias Carbuncle mask.

NEWBERRY: (*laughing*) Mm-hm.

WELLINGTON: I wouldn't be surprised.

EZRA: (*to herself*) Worse …

WELLINGTON: What?

EZRA: Gordias …

WELLINGTON: (*out*) I thought I heard her say –

NEWBERRY: What did you say?

(*Ezra looks up.*)

EZRA: I'm sorry?

NEWBERRY: You –

EZRA: What?

NEWBERRY: Oh –

EZRA: What?

WELLINGTON: (*out*) Vivian turned bright red.

EZRA: I'm sorry. I'm distracted.

WELLINGTON: It's all right.

EZRA: This whole mess has made me very very ...

WELLINGTON: Forget it.

EZRA: Oh God. Pauline ... You know what my life is? I read. All day, every day – read and write, research – in my office. I lecture to undergrads, meet with faculty, hold seminars, walk home – where I read some more. That's more or less what I did when I was in high school, and I did it again as an undergraduate and then again for my doctorate. It's probably what I'm going to do for the rest of my life. And I absolutely love it, so much, it's the perfect life for me. But God, it does seem small. My whole life. So small and unimportant. Providence, Rhode Island.

NEWBERRY: A lot of people feel that.

EZRA: When I discovered *Eternal Hydra* in Paris and realized what it was ... I can't even tell you. To read the entire history of civilization in his book. To see how he engaged with all the failures and compromises and abuses of history, the way he demanded accountability. And to see that Carbuncle needed my help, personally needed me to edit and annotate, to bring his work to light – can you imagine my joy? Six years. Rescuing those ninety-nine voices. Such moral work! So heroic!
 (*Pause.*) I should've never, Pauline ...

(*They sit in silence for a moment.*)

NEWBERRY: Do you remember Carbuncle's last letter to his cousin Daniel? From right before he died?

(*Ezra shakes her head no.*)

(*to Wellington*) You have his letters?

(*Wellington finds the collection and hands it to her. Newberry finds the letter.*)

Listen.
    (*reading*) 'April 12th, 1940. Dear Daniel … There's an interesting bit in the myth about the hydra's final head. No weapon could destroy it. Hercules had to rip it off the monster's body with his own bare hands. He buried it deep in the ground, rolling a gigantic boulder on top to keep it in the earth forever. Lovely image, yes? I must admit, I'm thinking of doing the same thing with my own final head.'

WELLINGTON: His last chapter?

NEWBERRY: (*reading*) 'But unlike Hercules, my dear Daniel, I do hope someday an inquisitive dog will come along to dig up that final head and carry it into town, for everyone to see its rotten remains.'

EZRA: His diary.

NEWBERRY: He wanted his readers to know.
    (*She looks at the galley copy of* Eternal Hydra.) Chapter seventy-two.

EZRA: Yes …

(*Wellington's office is fading away.*)

(*out*) Chapter seventy-two. New Orleans, Louisiana. 1866.

(*The scene has changed. Vivian has taken the book.*)

WELLINGTON: (*out*) By Gordias Carbuncle.

(*Wellington exits. Newberry has transformed into the Narrator from the chapter.*)

NARRATOR: (*out*) See, I got a story, and I'm gonna tell it now. All started in the spring of '62, that first May day in the tobacco when I saw lines of bluecoat and brass, muskets by their sides. Marching down the valley, a bunch of dusty troops together. Thought to myself: long last, the angels of vengeance descending. Gabriel's soldiers, straight from heaven. Turns out they were Yankees. Told us we were free and I said thank the Lord. I went down to New Orleans, my eyes so free and wide. Me and Q and Dixon and Lawful. Watching General Butler's wild boys hooting up the streets. But those ain't the glory days I'm here to tell. See, before the Lord's deliverance, back in days of bondage, I made shoes for Miss De Lancie. Had me a shed outside De Lancie's kitchen. Never used that skill my first years of freedom. Never had no luck with anything. But in the spring of '66, hungry, making rounds, I knocked on the hardwood door of a Canal St. Creole cobbler named Léon LaBas ...

(*Léon LaBas appears, played by the actor playing Wellington. The Narrator enters his 'shop.'*)

(*out*) Tall and dressed like a white man, skin the colour of caramel sugar. Wavy hair, a bit of kink. He spoke French and English both.

LABAS: You can make shoes?

NARRATOR: Yes, sir. Lord Almighty would've worn my shoes.

LABAS: A trade from your plantation?

NARRATOR: From De Lancie, up near Lafayette.
    (*out*) He checked me over and I must've looked a sight. My old brown dress all natty at the hem. Beat-up mistakes on my feet.

LABAS: You have no shoes for yourself.

NARRATOR: No, sir, no, I don't.

(*LaBas exits.*)

NARRATOR: (*out*) He went back into storage.

(*LaBas enters with a box of materials and tools.*)

(*out*) He comes out with a hide of leather. Awls, clams, a jigger. Tranchet and cork. Good thread and shoemaker's wax. And a last the size of my foot. Hands all to me and says:

LABAS: Take these tools and leather.
    (*He hands her the box.*) Make yourself a pair. If the shoe fits, as they say …

NARRATOR: But these here tools, they must be worth –

LABAS: You seem an honest woman. I trust you'll return.

NARRATOR: Oh yes, sir. I'll return.

LABAS: Very good.

NARRATOR: 'Til tomorrow.

LABAS: À demain.

NARRATOR: Yes, sir. All right.
   (*She exits the store.*) (*out*) I took them tools and left. Went working all the night. Clicking and blocking and closing. Cering, inseaming, too. Glazing and slicking when I was done. Made a sturdy pair of shoes, all for me. Even pinked some flowers on the vamp to show that Creole how fancy I can be. Came back next morning, new shoes on my feet.

(*She re-enters the store with the box of tools.*)

LABAS: Well, look who's returned.

NARRATOR: I brought your tools, sir. Everything, you can check.

LABAS: I needn't check.
   (*He looks her up and down, stopping at her shoes.*) My oh my ...

NARRATOR: Worked most the night.

LABAS: May I see them?

NARRATOR: Yes, sir.

(*She removes her shoes and hands them to LaBas. He studies them for a moment, then hands them back to her.*)

LABAS: You're hired.

NARRATOR: I am?

LABAS: Ten cents a pair.

NARRATOR: (*joyous*) Ten cents?

LABAS: We work on commission here.

NARRATOR: Thank you, sir!

LABAS: Start first thing in the morning.

NARRATOR: I'll be here.

(*She leaves the shop.*)

(*out*) Now I had myself a job, working the bench up front the store. Ten cents a pair! Monsieur LaBas used to sit there, in the back, big chair and big cigar, reading French poems and the *New Orleans Tribune*.

(*She has re-entered the shop,*)

LABAS: Mon Dieu! Look at this! Another Negro beaten for boarding a star car!

NARRATOR: (*out*) He'd call out news of the day.

LABAS: *Tribune's* editors are proposing full-scale Negro revolt. That's suicide, I say ...

NARRATOR: (*out*) I sure liked to hear him speak.

LABAS: All's well at the bench this morning?

NARRATOR: Yes, sir, mighty fine.

(*Narrator makes shoes. LaBas watches her.*)

LABAS: I enjoy watching you work.

NARRATOR: Thank you, Monsieur LaBas.

LABAS: You're talented, you know. Very elegant work.

NARRATOR: It's nothing, now. Just shoes for someone's feet.

LABAS: Don't you say that! You're a genuine artist.

NARRATOR: No, sir, no ...

LABAS: Yes! Never degrade your craft. You think God looks askance at His own creations? A great pair of shoes is much more than a thing of mere use. It's not so different from a painting by Michelangelo! It's an expression of yourself.

NARRATOR: Lord, you make me sound important.

LABAS: Well, I can see that making shoes is not just your livelihood. You're not some northern factory worker. You're a real artist.

NARRATOR: I try my best.

LABAS: What a pleasure to have you here.

(*LaBas touches her back, then watches her work.*)

NARRATOR: Can I ask you something, sir?

LABAS: Of course.

NARRATOR: Them two figures up there, above the door. I been looking at them.

LABAS: Ah, yes. They're the patron saints of our profession. Crispin and Crispinian. Brothers, sons of the Logrian king. Also known as the martyrs of Soissons. According to the most popular tales, they had the finest calf leathers flown to them each night by heaven's own archangels, for raw material.

NARRATOR: (*out*) He was educated like that. Always something to say.
　　　Crispinian, huh?

LABAS: Celebrated on the 25th of October. My wife and I have a little feast for family and friends. It's wonderful fun. I think you'll come this year.

NARRATOR: If you say, Monsieur LaBas.

LABAS: I do.

NARRATOR: Saints for shoemakers. Seems funny to me.

LABAS: Oh, we've more than saints for representation. Great poems and tales, too. Even plays written about us. You must read Thomas Dekker's wonderful work.

NARRATOR: Sure, I'll do that …

LABAS: I'll lend you my personal copy.

NARRATOR: All right.

LABAS: You have some hesitation.

NARRATOR: No, sir. No, I … no.

LABAS: Tell me.

NARRATOR: It ain't important.

LABAS: Please.

NARRATOR: I can't read.

LABAS: No, of course you can't.

NARRATOR: Course that seems peculiar to a man like you.

LABAS: It's not your fault. I'll have to teach you.

NARRATOR: You'd do that?

LABAS: Absolutely. After work.

(*He touches her.*) It would be my pleasure.

NARRATOR: Thank you, Monsieur LaBas.

LABAS: You're welcome.

NARRATOR: (*out*) I felt stupid, all right, but what else am I gonna do? I got my own pair of shoes, then this here job with good pay, now a chance to learn to read! And he was kind, Monsieur LaBas. So much kinder than …

(*She pauses.*) (*out*) Then comes the summer of '66. Monsieur LaBas started squirming, going on about 'Janus-face' Governor Wells and the upcoming convention. One day this Chicago white man comes in with his fancy lady friend. Man wore this three-piece suit, looked a Northerner for sure.

(*Henry Clay Warmoth and Sarah Briggs enter. They are played by the actors playing Carbuncle and Ezra. Narrator sits at her cobbler's bench.*)

(*out*) Monsieur LaBas jumps up to greet him, real excited, like he's someone important.

(*LaBas jumps up and meets Warmoth. Narrator watches from her work bench.*)

LABAS: Well, I'll be –

WARMOTH: Monsieur LaBas!

LABAS: Henry Warmoth! In New Orleans!

WARMOTH: Since March, in fact. The committee's kept me busy.

LABAS: How nice to see you again.

WARMOTH: I'd like you to meet Miss Sarah Briggs, youngest daughter of the esteemed Charles Briggs.

LABAS: Why, it's a pleasure.

BRIGGS: The pleasure is all mine.

(*LaBas pours a drink for Warmoth.*)

NARRATOR: (*out*) Monsieur LaBas turned to me and said:

LABAS: This here is Henry Clay Warmoth. The hope of Louisiana! Mr. Warmoth –

WARMOTH: How do you do.

LABAS: – is Louisiana's shadow delegate to the House of Representatives.

WARMOTH: That's right.

NARRATOR: (*out*) Says Warmoth, full of pride.

LABAS: He's representing our fine state up in Washington, D.C.

NARRATOR: Must be important work.

WARMOTH: Someone has to do it. And it's hardly all torture, I'll have you know.

LABAS: I'm sure there are those in Washington who find no one more attractive than a young Republican in the House of Representatives.

WARMOTH: Ah, but the ladies of our nation's capital are no match for the belles of New Orleans.

LABAS: That's for sure.

BRIGGS: Mr. Warmoth would never do anything to compromise the dignity of his position.

NARRATOR: (*out*) Says Miss Briggs, her eyes boring into that man.

WARMOTH: Yes, one must respect the austerity of the public realm.

BRIGGS: Dignity and pleasure are eternal foes. Except, of course, in New Orleans.

(*Briggs and Warmoth share a smile.*)

NARRATOR: (*out*) Those two made a perfect pair.

(*Briggs looks around the shop and eventually notices Narrator's shoes.*)

WARMOTH: Now, I came to tell you about the state convention Governor Wells is planning for July 30th.

LABAS: I was just reading about it.

WARMOTH: It will be an historic day for your people.

NARRATOR: How come?

WARMOTH: It's our intention to grant the Negro his legal right to vote.

BRIGGS: By the order of Governor Wells. Educated and freedman alike.

WARMOTH: But never the ladies, thank the Lord!

NARRATOR: Governor Wells wants us to vote?

WARMOTH: Want has nothing to do with it. He's been pushed into the corner. Without the coloured vote, he's sure to lose the next election.

NARRATOR: You don't say …

WARMOTH: It's the beginning of your triumph! Once suffrage is attained, the Negro shall, at long last, have the historical power to free himself. For he's intelligent, our Negro. I have always said as much. He will ponder his options in a rational fashion then offer his voice, and his vote, to the ablest man of our times. And I have no doubt the Negro will elect a Herculean soul for his governor. A man with the intelligence and skill to represent the true will of Louisiana.

NARRATOR: A man like you, Mr. Warmoth?

WARMOTH: One never knows …

BRIGGS: Mr. Warmoth is too modest. He is indeed such a soul. I wouldn't put it past our Hercules here to save our poor state all by himself.

WARMOTH: Now, Miss Briggs, not even Hercules had to face your Southern Democrat.

BRIGGS: Well, Henry, you'll just have to slay that particular beast one head at a time.

NARRATOR: (*out*) Them two smiling at each other.

WARMOTH: Slaying monsters is just one of the many things Sarah learned in her studies up at Holyoke.

LABAS: I see.

WARMOTH: Along with certain political positions not quite appreciated by her father.

BRIGGS: Indeed, Mr. Briggs and I held conflicting opinions about the proper state of the Union during the war.

LABAS: Oh dear.

BRIGGS: He now stands corrected.

(*LaBas laughs.*)

LABAS: Delightful!

WARMOTH: Charles Briggs has introduced me to all the men of stature in our state.

BRIGGS: And who, Mr. Warmoth, introduced you to Charles Briggs?

(*LaBas laughs.*)

WARMOTH: His daughter. Yes, indeed.

BRIGGS: I will have my rightful place.

LABAS: Louisiana will be forever in your debt.

(*Warmoth picks up his hat and gloves, prepares to leave.*)

WARMOTH: So. The Mechanics' Institute on Dryades.

LABAS: Of course.

WARMOTH: Nine in the morning, July 30th. We need supporters on the street!

(*Warmoth and Briggs exit.*)

NARRATOR: (*out*) Couple weeks by, I'm working Monday morning, July 30th, when Monsieur LaBas hurries in.

(*LaBas enters the shop.*)

(*out*) He's dressed up in his suit, hair back flat as it can be. He sees me cering and says:

LABAS: What is that you're wearing?

NARRATOR: My usual.

LABAS: Well, it won't do.

NARRATOR: Won't do for what?

LABAS: Hurry home, before it's too late! Dress your Sunday's best. We're closing shop today.

NARRATOR: 'Cause of the convention?

LABAS: Yes, of course. You're coming to the Institute with me.

NARRATOR: (*out*) How I wished my Sunday best was better than what it was.
    (*She finishes working.*) I suppose I'll go like this.

LABAS: You should dress for the occasion.

NARRATOR: Well, all right. If you say …
    (*out*) But he had something else in mind.

(*LaBas reveals a dress decorated with a magnolia print.*)

LABAS: Here you go. Put on this.

NARRATOR: Oh Lord!

(*He hands her the dress.*)

LABAS: You'll be paid today as if you made ten pairs of shoes.

NARRATOR: Monsieur LaBas …

LABAS: Put on that dress.

NARRATOR: (*out*) I did. Right there.

(*As the Narrator puts on her dress, LaBas approaches and rubs his hand over her newly showing, pregnant belly. She finishes dressing.*)

(*out*) Was it ever fine. Had a big magnolia print. Nothing like it I ever owned. I never looked so good. Never felt so good neither. Monsieur LaBas was smiling grand.

LABAS: Lovely.

NARRATOR: Thank you.

LABAS: How lovely. I'm reluctant to leave.
(*He kisses her cheek.*) Gonna be a beautiful mother.
(*He steps away.*) The procession will come up Canal and make its way towards the Institute. Let's go and join them.

NARRATOR: All right.

(*LaBas exits. Narrator stands alone.*)

(*out*) We left shop and saw the procession. A whole group of black folks, men, women and kids, dressed and marching up to Dryades, waving Union flags. Lots of army mixed in. Black troops marching to the beat of fife and drum. They carried guns and clubs, in case of trouble. We met that crowd, me and Monsieur LaBas. And I ran into Lawful there, that old friend of mine from De Lancie plantation. He wore his bluecoat uniform from the Native Guards. There I was, so proud, marching up Canal. A coloured Union soldier to the left of me, an educated Creole to the right. Walking right on up to get the vote. Might just be my best few minutes … followed by my worst. We come to the Institute and Monsieur LaBas goes inside, 'cause he's part of that convention. Me and Lawful staying out front. There were all kind of skirmishes around, white folks jeering and calling names. Nothing all that new. Then a group of them come out swinging clubs. Shooting guns. Turned a full force riot. We got to running, but city police were 'round the corner, all that time, lying in wait. And now what do you think they do? Start shooting with them others. We turned on back towards the Institute but there ain't no where to go. A policeman shot my Lawful in the back of his head, while running. Slumped like animal slaughter and hit the stones, losing life. I stooped down to help, but I got kicked in the side of my head. So I made way back to the store, waiting for Monsieur LaBas to come. Lawful's blood on my magnolias. Brand new thing and I ruined it less than a day. And Monsieur LaBas, never coming.

(*She sits at the cobbler's bench.*) (*out*) Next day I'm at shop, cobbling double speed. Whole city ain't moving, under martial law, but I got orders to fill, make my pay. The door opens and who walks in?

(*Henry Warmoth enters, trying to hide his face.*)

(*out*) That Henry Clay Warmoth, in his three-piece suit. Hiding from folks out on the street. Inside he shows himself.

(*Warmoth looks at Narrator. He has a big black eye, other bruises.*)

(*to Warmoth*) Oh Lord, please say no …

WARMOTH: I'm sorry.

NARRATOR: Please say no.

(*Warmoth nods.*)

NARRATOR: Léon …

WARMOTH: They ambushed us inside. Blocked the entrances and stormed the Institute. Léon was caught in a crossfire. I'm quite certain he passed away quickly.

NARRATOR: How come you got out?

WARMOTH: Hid in a closet. Kept my head down. I found a moment to slip away.

NARRATOR: (*She crosses herself.*) Lord have mercy on his soul.

WARMOTH: Amen. I'm afraid I can't stay in Louisiana. I must keep off the streets. Not safe for me, here. But I felt you should be informed of Léon's death.

NARRATOR: That's kind of you, Mr. Warmoth.
(*out*) He makes about to leave. Then he turns to me and says:

WARMOTH: You realize, of course, I'll never abandon the fine people of Louisiana. I shall return. I understand your people's legacy, all that you've endured. And I have a vision for your productive future. As for yesterday's horrors, I will personally lobby General Sheridan and President Johnson for immediate action. I'll nail those Confederate backs to the wall. Laws will change. The Negro will receive his vote. And once again I'll stand tall in New Orleans, bringing prosperity back to its glorious people.

NARRATOR: Yes, sir.

WARMOTH: Well, then. Good luck.

NARRATOR: Good luck to you.

(*Warmoth notices her shoes.*)

Is something … ?

WARMOTH: No, no, not at all. Just, those are very lovely shoes.

NARRATOR: Thank you, sir.

WARMOTH: Whose handy work?

NARRATOR: I made 'em myself.

WARMOTH: Did you, really?

NARRATOR: My very first day on this here job.

WARMOTH: Remarkable.

NARRATOR: I've been told shoes can be important as a painting on someone's wall.

WARMOTH: Yes, yes …

NARRATOR: Don't know if that's true.

WARMOTH: By any chance are they for sale? I would like to give Miss Briggs, the young lady of my acquaintance, a gift before my departure. She has done so much for me. And those are precisely in her style.

NARRATOR: I don't know …

WARMOTH: Such reticence.

NARRATOR: First time I ever made a pair for myself.

WARMOTH: Ah, yes, sentimental value. That old demon. I understand. (*Pause.*) It's unfortunate, without Monsieur LaBas, this shop won't be operational much longer.

NARRATOR: No, sir.

WARMOTH: Your income's sure to decrease.

NARRATOR: Yes, sir.

WARMOTH: It's terrible for you.

NARRATOR: I love this job.

WARMOTH: Well, so be it. Hard times for everyone. Who knows? Maybe you'll find another cobbler's position. I wish you the best of luck.

(*Warmoth doesn't leave.*)

NARRATOR: If you want them shoes, Mr. Warmoth, they're for sale. Ten cents.

WARMOTH: One dollar, I suspect, buys you time to find other employment.

NARRATOR: I don't know. It might.

(*Warmoth takes out a bill.*)

WARMOTH: For some reason, the U.S. bank at the end of Royal always has the freshest currency.

(*He gives her the money. She hands her shoes to him.*)

I'm certain Miss Briggs will be thrilled.

NARRATOR: Yes, sir, I'm sure she will.

WARMOTH: Thank you.

NARRATOR: Uh-huh.

WARMOTH: Goodbye.

NARRATOR: Goodbye, Mr. Warmoth.

WARMOTH: Although I'm quite sure we'll meet again.

NARRATOR: Yes, sir. I suppose we will.

WARMOTH: Until then.

NARRATOR: Until then.

(*Warmoth exits the shop. Sarah Briggs appears, and Warmoth approaches her.*)

WARMOTH: Miss Briggs.

BRIGGS: Mr. Warmoth. You're leaving New Orleans?

WARMOTH: I am.

BRIGGS: With your tail between your legs. Have I overestimated you?

(*Warmoth smiles.*)

WARMOTH: I brought you a parting gift.

(*Warmoth offers her the shoes.*)

BRIGGS: For me?

(*They share a smile. She takes the shoes, admires them.*)

BRIGGS: Thank you, Henry.

WARMOTH: You're welcome. Will you try them on?

BRIGGS: Yes. In the governor's mansion at your inauguration.

WARMOTH: Right. Of course.

NARRATOR: (*out*) That was my life and it was good. Summer of
'66, before the riot of New Orleans. Working for my pay and
then paying my own way. Now I can't get work, least not
making shoes. That Henry Warmoth, though, that one I had
my eye on, he's governor of Louisiana.

(*Warmoth puts the shoes on Briggs' feet. They stand together, apart
from Narrator.*)

Henry Warmoth. Right from the start that Northerner had his
eye on us coloured folk. Made sure to keep us friends. Oh, he
had himself a plan all along. When he ran for governor all our
men voted for him. And you know, sometimes I suppose I
would've voted for that Warmoth, too – if a woman could vote.
'Cause he's the reality of New Orleans. White man's the one
who speaks, here. White man's the only one who gets heard.
Better to give him my voice than keep it useless for myself.

(*Warmoth exits. Briggs becomes Ezra. She listens to Narrator.*)

One time I took my daughter down to Jackson Square to hear
that Henry Warmoth give a speech. 'If you give the Negroes
an opportunity,' he said, 'they can do almost anything. Like the
Negress cobbler I met before the riot of '66, who made my
wife a pair of shoes as beautiful as a painting on someone's
wall.' To hear him say that. Felt like me up there, onstage. Not
him at all. You never know. Might just be my voice coming
from his mouth.

Acknowledgements

Thank you:

To Andrey Tarasiuk, who commissioned and directed this play as a one-act for the Stratford Festival's fiftieth anniversary.

To Stephen Ouimette, Chick Reid and Paul Soles. I have incorporated many of their suggestions. Thanks also to Roy Surette and the late Richard Monette.

To David Ferry, Liisa Repo-Martell, Karen Robinson, Sam Malkin and Merissa Tordjman, brilliant collaborators and friends. Their love and attention pervade this script. It's been a great privilege to work with them.

To my family and friends: Joram and Lona Piatigorsky, Auran Piatigorsky, Tonje Vetleseter, Stephen and Sheila Roth, Justin Adler, Ben Ehrenreich, Erik Rutherford, Sheila Heti, David Wharnsby, Kristen Thomson, Hussain Amarshi, Ben and Diana Winters, Brian Current, Jenn Stephenson, Sean Robb, Tom McCamus, Annie Keating, Kim Hawkins, Kish Iqbal, John Elko, Peter and Dara Edney, Nicolas Billon, Greg Campbell, Michael and Elizabeth Varet, Evan Drachman, Daniel Brooks, John Mighton and the many others who have helped, in some way, with this play.

To Alana Wilcox, Evan Munday, Christina Palassio and everyone at Coach House Press.

To my children, Sivan, Dalia and Reuben.

To Ava, my beloved.

And to Chris Abraham, for his brilliant dramaturgy and perfect direction.

About the Playwright

Anton Piatigorsky's plays include *The Kabbalistic Psychoanalysis of Adam R. Tzaddik*, *Mysterium Tremendum*, *The Offering* and *Easy Lenny Lazmon and the Great Western Ascension*. His frequent collaborations with director Chris Abraham have travelled across Canada and the United States, receiving awards for writing and direction. He is the recipient of a Dora Mavor Moore award for best new play, and the 2005 Elinore and Lou Siminovitch Protégé Award for playwrighting. Anton's other work includes the libretto for *Airline Icarus*, a chamber opera by composer Brian Current, an adaptation of S. Anski's *The Dybbuk*, and a collection of short stories about dictators as teenagers.

Typeset in My Underwood and Adobe Jenson
Printed and bound at the Coach House on bpNichol Lane, May 2009

Edited and designed by Alana Wilcox
Back cover photo of David Ferry by Colin O'Connor

Coach House Books
401 Huron Street on bpNichol Lane
Toronto, Ontario M5S 2G5

416 979 2217
800 367 6360

mail@chbooks.com
www.chbooks.com